Hard Target

G. Beahan

Breakwater
100 Water Street
P.O. Box 2188
St. John's, Newfoundland
A1C 6E6

Cover illustration by Angela King-Harris.

Canadian Cataloguing in Publication Data

Beahan, G.
    Hard Target
    ISBN 0-920911-91-9

I. Title

PS8553.E23H37   1990   C813'.54   C90-097551-2
PR9199.3.B42H37   1990

*The Publisher gratefully acknowledges the financial support
of the Cultural Affairs Division, Department of Municipal
and Provincial Affairs, Government of Newfoundland and
Labrador, and The Canada Council which has helped make
this publication possible.*

I

Bannister struggled out of an uncomfortable doze, only half conscious that he had been awakened by the pilot's voice blaring too loudly from the cabin speakers. His mouth was dry and the arm he had been leaning on was numb and tingling.

He stretched and yawned as a stewardess delivered the usual instructions— also too loud— about buckling seat belts and placing chairs and chair tables in a fully upright position, then repeated the whole thing more rapidly and fluidly in French. Bannister looked at his watch, mentally adding time zones. One-thirty...no, there was this crazy half hour thing.... Two a.m. Two hours late.

The stout, red-faced man in the next seat was bent over double, panting with the exertion of getting his shoes back on. When he straightened up, his face was a dangerous shade of purple.

"What was the pilot saying?" Bannister inquired. "I was asleep, there, I guess...."

The purple-faced man glowered. "He said we're going down to have a look. If he can land, we land. If he can't, we go to Gander."

"Oh," said Bannister. "Yeah. What happens if we go to Gander?"

"Nothing good." The man was now struggling with his shirt button and tugging his tie into position.

"Maybe we wait around the airport for an hour while they find our baggage and round up some taxis to take us to a hotel. By that time, it's about four a.m. Then they wake us up about six and haul us back out to the airport." He glared at Bannister as though holding him personally responsible.

"Or," he went on, "maybe we wait around the airport for an hour while they round up some school buses with seats a foot wide, then they put us aboard and haul us into St. John's."

"Ah," said Bannister. "How long does that take?"

"About five hours," the man replied grimly. "If you're lucky."

"Sounds like you've been here before." Bannister began a jocular chuckle, but under his seat-mate's accusing glare abandoned it and cleared his throat instead.

"Every year," the man said, "I say the same thing. I'm not going to St. John's in the spring, I say. And here I am. Every year."

The pitch of the engine rose and fell in irregular pattern, the cabin bucked and shuddered, hydraulics whined. Suddenly, in the black, wet square of the window, grey-haloed lights appeared, surprisingly close, and seconds later the aircraft hit the runway with a bone-jarring thump, bounced once, steadied, and began to decelerate with a roar. A group of passengers gave a ragged round of applause and a few ironic cheers.

"They seem happy," said Bannister.

"I guess they've been to Gander before."

Waiting for his bags among the yawning passengers and the handful of subdued greeters, Bannister tried to recall something he had half heard in the pilot's announcement as he was waking up. Something incongruous had nearly caught his attention, but his mind was still too fuzzed with sleep to bring it into focus. Only when he stepped out of the terminal building did he come fully awake as a bitter wind lashed a handful of wet snow across his cheek.

The pilot had been describing the weather on the ground. Bannister looked around in disbelief. The parking lot lights seemed to be shrouded in fog, and heavy, wet flakes were driving through the murk. Bannister shivered and pulled his light raincoat tight around his neck as a driver in a parka hustled him toward a cab.

Finally checked in at the Hotel Newfoundland, he sat gloomily on the bed and examined his hand-tooled western boots. Both on getting into and out of the taxi he had stepped in six inches of slush. Three a.m. local time. It would be— what, one o'clock in Houston? No, twelve-thirty. The malaise he had felt on the airplane had not left him. In fact, it had got worse. He picked up the telephone and dialled. On the fourth ring he got an answer.

"Hello, Al," Bannister said. "Not in bed yet?"

"Bronco! Where are you? Listen, is something wrong?"

"Al," Bannister said quietly, "do you know what it's doing here?"

"What the hell...?"

"It's snowing, Al. It is the twenty-second of May, Al, and it's snowing. The temperature is zero degrees by the Celsius scale, which would be about...."

"Bronco," Al broke in, "just switch to Mode One, will you, so's we can talk?" Bannister sighed. He picked up one of his briefcases, snapped it open, slid the telephone handset into a padded receptacle, flicked a switch, and picked up the handset that was clipped into the briefcase lid.

"Scrambler. Mode One," he said. "Reading?"

There was a crackle from the earphone and Al's voice came again, sounding metallic and more distant. "All right, Bannister, what is it with this goddamn weather report? What are you calling me for?"

"Al," Bannister said. "I don't want this job."

"Listen, are you drunk, for God's sake?"

"Al, you know I ain't a drinker...."

"Yeah." The tinny voice was louder. "You ain't been a nut-case, neither. Up till now. What do you mean, you don't want the job?"

"I just don't want it," Bannister said. "It feels all wrong. There's something about this place.... I've just got this feeling that it's not for me. I'd like you to get somebody else for it, Al."

"Bronco...."

"Not only is it snowing, but it's foggy and the wind is blowing like hell, all at once. That ain't natural, Al. Not anytime, but especially not on the twenty-second of May."

"For Chrissakes, Bannister, you're in Canada, aren't you? What did you expect? Palm trees? You've been in Canada before...."

"I've been in Calgary, Toronto, places like that. This ain't places like that. They put six people in a taxi and drive them home all over town before bringing me to my hotel. The driver talked the whole way, and I couldn't understand a word he said...."

"Goddamn it, Bannister, what's the matter with you? You've spent half your life in places where they don't talk English. Most of the cab-drivers anyplace don't talk English these days."

"This guy *was* talking English, Al. I think."

Al grunted impatiently.

"I get to the hotel, and I've got to stand in line with a bunch of other people who've also been driving around in taxis, taking people home. The desk clerk says they're short-handed because it's a holiday, and everybody's gone trouting."

"So? People have been known to go fishing on a holiday."

"In the snow, for God's sake? So I say, 'What holiday?' and he says, 'The twenty-fourth of May.' What the hell kind of an answer is that? Especially when it's the twenty-second.

"Anyways, Al, I don't like this whole thing. I've got a real bad feeling about it, like a premonition or something. There's a flight out of here in about four hours, and I want to be on it."

"You can't do that, Bronco. You...."

"Come on, Al, give me a break. There's no tearing hurry to get set up here, is there? You could get somebody else— Lawrence, or Harrison, or...."

"Listen, Bronco," Al said in a tight voice, "I'll tell you what I'm going to do. I'm going to hang up this phone in about sixty seconds, and I'm going to go to bed. It must be— what— three o'clock in the morning up there? You just have a shower and think things over. Like, for instance, where your pay cheque comes from every month. Like, you're still paying alimony to— whatsername— Alice, right? Like your kid, there— you still got him in that military academy in Louisiana? Do you pay for that by the year, or the quarter, or how?"

"Al...."

"Have a good sleep, Bronco. We'll talk tomorrow."

Bannister pulled the hotel telephone out of the briefcase and dropped it on its cradle, then wandered disconsolately to the window, where soggy snow was gathering in little clumps and gliding sideways across the pane, driven by the implacable wind.

II

The view from the window next morning was so different that the hotel might have been magically transported during the night to another country. The sun burned in a sky of almost unnatural depth and blueness, the colourful wooden buildings of the Battery steamed merrily like so many tea-kettles, and the only signs of the events of the night before were a few rapidly shrinking puddles and a fluffy, white, innocent-looking heap of fog retreating from the harbour mouth.

Bannister felt much better. He now regretted the call to Houston. Must have been indigestion or something, he thought. I'll call him later and square it. He ordered a hearty breakfast, then snapped open a panel on the lid of his suitcase, withdrew a heavy folder, and settled down to read.

He had barely skimmed the first few pages, with which he was already familiar, before he was surprised by a knock on the door. He was even more surprised on opening it to be greeted by name.

The doorway was nearly filled by a broad, fleshy figure in a breezy checked top-coat, with the smile and the voice of a television pitchman. "Mr. Bannister?" the figure beamed. "Mind if I call you Bronco? God bless you, my friend. Welcome to St. John's. Isn't it a lovely day?"

The voice was unmistakably of the American South. Bannister shook a large, damp hand, and somehow the visitor was inside the room. "Yeah," Bannister said. "Uh...?"

"Jarvis, Bronco. Pastor Virgil T. Jarvis of the Emmanuel Church of the Living Gospel. Hope to see you there on Sunday morning, for a bit of good ol' down home preaching." He flashed the pitchman's toothy smile. "Now, if I was a betting man, which thank the good Lord I'm not, I'd just lay a wager you're wondering to yourself, what's a preacher-man from Alabama doing 'way up here?"

Bannister was about to allow that the thought had crossed his mind, but Jarvis did not wait for confirmation. "Well, I'll tell you, my friend. I came here some years ago in the service of our country. I was doing my hitch in the good ol' U.S. Navy, and the Lord saw to it that I was sent here to the base at Argentia. You know of it, my friend?"

"Uh, yeah," Bannister said."I...."

"I was young then, my friend. I was headstrong. I didn't much like the idea of spending my time on some cold rock away out in the Atlantic Ocean. But the good Lord had plans for me. I found good people here, my friend. Good, simple people, hungry for God's word. I felt the Call. So when my hitch was up I came back to them, my friend. But this time I came in another Service— the Service of the Lord."

This was in fact a reasonably accurate account, though it left a number of significant matters unmentioned. Jarvis had spent a tour of duty at Argentia, and he had returned to Newfoundland with one of the American evangelical road-shows that tour the Canadian hinterland in the summers. And he had stayed on to set up his own church. Where the money had come from to set it up was a question that no one had so far thought to ask.

With his beefy good looks, shock of dark hair greying at the temples, commanding presence and resonant voice, he had attracted a sizable congregation of local fans of the American evangelists seen on cable television, as well as a number of his fellow countrymen involved in offshore oil exploration.

A natural showman, he had quickly begun to take advantage of every opportunity for appearing on the local media to denounce moral decay, alcohol, rock music, and permissiveness in education. St. John's journalists had learned to count on him to enliven those occasional days when automobile accidents, international disasters, and political scandals were in short supply.

"Yes, indeed," Jarvis went on, without a pause. "In the Service of the Lord." He flashed his broad smile again. "Of course, I serve my country, too. *Our* country, I should say."

For Bannister, a decidedly unwelcome light was beginning to dawn.

"Yeah," he said. "Right."

That is not exactly brilliant repartee, Bronco, he told himself. This snake-oil salesman has caught you with your pants down around your ankles, and all you can say is "right"?

"Right," he said again, in spite of himself. "Yeah. Serve your country. Ah...is that in an official capacity...?" Jarvis put his large hand on Bannister's shoulder. "That all depends, my friend, on your point of view. There used to be an American consulate here, until a few years ago, but there isn't one now. I act as a kind of unofficial consul, you might say. I like to welcome people like yourself...."

"Unofficially?" Bannister said.

"Well, yes, my friend. You might say that. I have no official standing as far as the government here is concerned, of course." He kept his hand on Bannister's shoulder. "But our own government does take notice of my efforts. Yes, they do indeed. They do appreciate the small services I can render." The skin around his pale blue eyes crinkled with another warm smile, but Bannister noted that the eyes themselves had a disconcertingly direct and penetrating stare. "I'm surprised you haven't...ah... heard my name."

Yeah, thought Bannister. Right. The sinking feeling of the previous night was back. I am definitely not starting off on the right foot here, he thought. I wonder if I'm getting sick or something? With considerable effort, he prevented himself from saying "right" again.

"Sure," he said. "As a matter of fact, I did read something...I...ah...got in kind of late last night...didn't make the connection right away. Haven't quite got myself oriented...."

"I understand, my friend. Your flight was delayed in Halifax, I'm told. And then, my goodness, you nearly didn't get in here at all! The good Lord does sometimes send us some trying weather. But you'll get used to it." The tone was soothing, and he squeezed Bannister's shoulder companionably, but the pale eyes were still steadily levelled. "You get yourself oriented. Come around to the church and see us. Why, I've got an Assistant Pastor from down around your way. He'd be mighty pleased to make your acquaintance. Mighty pleased."

One of the features of Jarvis's church was that he had a regular succession of Assistant Pastors. All were Americans and most of them were a little older than one would expect ministers in training to be, men who had apparently, like Jarvis himself, heard the Call after a period of military service, or something like it. They arrived at intervals from Virginia or Texas or obscure missions abroad, stayed for a few months, and moved on. Most had a trim, athletic look about them. The current incumbent was drawing overflow crowds of teenagers to Wednesday night services by giving a Karate demonstration while Pastor Jarvis delivered a rousing sermon on "Kicking Hell Out of the Devil."

"Yeah," said Bannister. "Thanks."

"Now, my friend, if you should want my help in any way, you just call on me. I'm easy to find." He gave Bannister's shoulder a last squeeze and chuckled warmly. "And I'd be mighty proud to see you in church on Sunday morning. Mighty proud. Now, you have yourself a real nice day, you hear?" And Jarvis stepped out into the hall.

"Yeah. That's great. Thanks." Bannister closed the door and leaned on it for a moment, shaking his head. Could I be getting too old for this business? he thought.

He ordered another pot of coffee, picked up the folder he had been reading from, sighed, shook his head again, and flipped through the pages until he found the entry that confirmed what had begun to dawn on him shortly after Jarvis had called him by name. "Shit," he said.

It was not the simple fact that Jarvis was an agent of the CIA that bothered him. There was bound to be one, and Bannister would have met him— or her— shortly, anyway. The trouble was in the way the meeting had happened. Normally, these matters followed a rigorous, if informal, protocol.

Someone in Bannister's position, arriving on a new station, would be expected to get in touch with the local CIA operative as a matter of course. But members of Bannister's organization were always at pains to ensure that these contacts did not have the appearance of checking in or gaining clearance from the Agency, or in any way acknowledging inferior status. Usually they would wait a day or two to establish their independence, and most CIA operatives went along in the interests of harmonious working relationships.

And that wasn't all. Going by the book, someone in Bannister's position would have read, memorized, and destroyed his briefing kit before ever leaving Houston, and been fully informed on all facets of the local scene. But on routine jobs in English-speaking and friendly territory, practice allowed some slack.

Except in cases of emergency, it was standard procedure to goof off a bit before leaving home, wait until you got on station, then put your feet up for a couple of days while getting briefed. The CIA spooks knew that, too. The only reason why Jarvis would have called on him without hardly giving him time to have breakfast was that he wanted to catch him off base: a bit of petty one-upmanship that did not augur well for any professional relationship they might have in the future.

Bannister slapped the file down in exasperation. He now seriously regretted that early-morning phone call to Houston. Anybody who'd go to such trouble to score a cheap point like that would be certain to report it, and the boys at Jarvis's home base in Langley would lose no time in using the incident to get a rise out of Al. It was the sort of petty put-down that they would love. Bannister winced when he thought of Al's all-too-predictable reaction.

His second pot of coffee arrived, and he sipped morosely as he picked up the file again and began to read. Outside the window an ominous looking pile of dark cloud was beginning to climb into the brilliant sky.

The coffee was still warm when the telephone rang.

Yeah, thought Bannister. Right. Resignedly, he picked up his scrambler as he went to answer it, and was ready for Al's chilly greeting.

"Morning Bronco. Mode One." Bannister attached the scrambler. "How's the weather?" Al inquired.

"It's okay. Look, Al...."

"No snow? Have a good night's sleep?"

"Yeah. Great. Thanks." Bannister kicked the upholstered chair in front of him.

"Good," said Al, his voice rising. "Because now I want you to tell me what the hell this is all about. In twenty-five words or less."

"Well, it's.... It's kind of hard to explain. Like I told you last night...."

"This morning."

"Yeah. Well, anyways, like I told you, there's something about this place.... It's nothing you can put your finger on, but I felt it right away when I got here. I don't know...I just figured...."

"I never knew you to go in for mysterious feelings, Bronco. You're too good a field man. One of the best. That's why I sent you up there. That's a straightforward job, but it's important. I want it done right. And I figured Bronco Bannister is the man to do it."

"Yeah," said Bannister. "Thanks."

"Don't mention it. Because now I ain't so sure any more. You've got me scared. Even the best of us can crack up, you know. It's nothing to be ashamed of. This is a high-pressure line of work. So if you got problems, you can get help."

Bannister felt a thin film of perspiration break out on his forehead. This was not at all what he had in mind when he had placed his impetuous late-night call. He had been thinking of re-assignment. The last thing he wanted was "help." That would mean going back to Houston, endless interviews with psychiatrists with Internal Security hanging on every word, probably followed by a desk job for the foreseeable future with piles of paperwork and no expense account. At best.

"Christ, no, Al!" he said quickly. "It's nothing like that!" He kicked the chair again, hard enough to bruise his toe. "I was just thinking that maybe another job... some place else...."

"I don't think so, Bronco. I think you'd better come in and let the shrinks look you over. I can...."

Bannister pulled the pillow off his bed and kicked it across the room. This is ridiculous, he thought. Last night I was demanding to get out of here. This morning I'm about to go down on my knees and beg him to let me stay. Maybe I *am* cracking up.

"Come on, Al," he said with forced jocularity. "Lighten up. I wasn't serious. It's a bit of a shock to walk into a snow-storm at the end of May, that's all. You said it yourself— I'm a good field man. I got a good record. I'll be fine."

"I don't know," Al said. "It wouldn't be easy to replace you just now, but...."

Bannister relaxed a little. "Yeah, I know. Listen, don't give it another thought." Then he tensed again. There was one more bit of delicate business to be got through before the conversation was over. "Funny sort of place, this," he said, trying very hard to sound casual.

"Yeah, so it seems. Only I ain't laughing a whole lot yet."

"The...ah...the Company guy seems like a real bastard."

Al's voice was quick and wary. "The Company guy? That asshole Jarvis? You been in touch with him already? What for?"

"Well," said Bannister carefully, "the thing is, he kind of got in touch with me. Seems like a real bird-dog."

There was an ominous silence at the other end of the line. "You know something, Bronco," Al said finally. "You said you had a funny feeling? Well, I'm starting to get a funny feeling myself."

"How's that, Al?"

"I'm starting to get a funny goddamn feeling that I know just what's going on up there. I got a feeling you spent the last week tomcatting around Houston with that little bimbo with the big knockers from down on the third floor instead of reading your goddamn kit. And then you get out there with no briefing, and you phone me with goddamn weather reports instead of doing your goddamn job. And this goddamn Company jerk drops in on you and you don't even goddamn well know who he is! Now, how's that for a funny goddamn feeling?"

Bannister held the phone away from his ear, picturing the secretaries outside Al's office door exchanging glances and rolling their eyes.

"You ain't cracking up, Bannister, you're goddamn slacking off!"

Bannister didn't answer.

"Now, you listen to me, Bannister, and listen good. There is nothing on this earth I'd like to do better than to haul your ass out of there and give you a job shuffling paper in the goddamn basement for the next eighty-five years. But I'm not going to do it. Because if I do it, you know what I'm going to hear from those faggots in Virginia? 'What happened to your boy in Newfoundland?' I'm going to hear, 'I hope our boy didn't scare him off,' I'm going to hear." Al delivered these imagined taunts in a mincing, sneering falsetto.

"Now, get this, Bannister. You're going to stay right where you are. You're going to do that job, and you're going to do it right. You are not going to give that spook preacher one teensy little thing to criticize. You are going to run a textbook operation, all the way. And maybe— just maybe— I won't send you to Tierra del Fuego when it's done. Maybe."

Al slammed down the phone. Bannister lay back on the bed and pulled the remaining pillow over his head.

III

In spite of the unfortunate beginning, when Bannister finally got to work he moved with sure speed and skill. As Al had said, he was a good field man.

He read and absorbed the briefing kit, then destroyed most of it. He made a few calls and introduced himself to a few people. Within twenty-four hours of his visit with Pastor Jarvis he was being shown through empty offices by eager real estate agents, and by that afternoon he had selected a large and expensive suite, centrally located on Duckworth Street, and started making arrangements with decorators, furniture and equipment suppliers, and the telephone company.

The locals did not seem to be used to moving at the pace he set, and at first they were somewhat misled by his informal, casual-seeming manner, but somehow they found themselves promising to do things— and doing them— with a dispatch that surprised even themselves.

News of all this activity travelled quickly through the city's business community. For fifteen years or more they had been on a roller coaster of anticipation and disappointment generated by exploration for oil and gas on the Grand Banks a hundred-odd miles offshore. There had been the booms of speculation when housing prices skyrocketed, strange buildings were built and stranger ones planned, expensive and unlikely specialty shops popped up like exotic plants, and everybody expected to make a fortune overnight.

But there had also been the dips and downturns when world oil prices fell, the rigs stopped drilling, and the busiest people in town were sign painters producing cheap paper banners for Going Out of Business sales. The downtown area had become a weird mixture of shiny glass office buildings and empty store fronts.

Still, the survivors had not entirely lost heart. The big bonanza was still out there waiting, and the setting up of what looked like a pretty big outfit of petroleum industry consultants was a decidedly hopeful sign. A ripple of cautious excitement ran along Water Street and up the hill behind.

The solid, permanent look of the new company's offices was observed with approval, and everybody was delighted to cooperate with the big, friendly American manager. "A real pro," they told each other. "He's worked in the oil business all over the place. If they're putting out all that money to set up in St. John's— well, they must know something!"

This assessment was truer than anyone who expressed it could imagine. The man they were talking about was more of a pro than they had any idea, and he and his employers knew things that would have made their heads spin.

Lee Edward Bannister had been born on a moderately prosperous south Texas farm that in later life he tended to promote to a ranch, since that seemed to be what people expected of Texans. He grew up to play football well enough for a scholarship to a small agricultural and mechanical college where he earned the nickname of Bronco for escapades both on and off the field, annoyed his parents by majoring not in agriculture but in engineering, and took a mediocre degree.

This led to a series of undistinguished oil industry jobs in Louisiana, Mexico, and assorted other places.

After a time it became clear to certain keen-eyed observers that although he was not up to much as a technician, the genial young engineer had potential they could use. He was affable and friendly, and handled people well, but at the same time he was a bit of a loner. He did not seem to be overburdened with scruples. He had a good memory and a knack for finding things out and getting things done while appearing to be looking the other way.

One day, one of the watchers took him out to lunch and introduced him to a fellow named Al.

It turned out to be a long lunch. The talk began with some minor problems on Bannister's current job but quickly went on to a more general discussion of the problems of big organizations. His hosts, who seemed to be consultants of some sort, were full of ideas on the subject. But they were picking up the tab, so Bannister ate his filet, listened politely, and tried not to yawn.

"You take the dinosaurs," said the one called Al, waving his fork. "They got so goddamn big, they had to spend all their time just staying alive. All's they could do was eat and shit and make baby dinosaurs; anything else, they couldn't handle it. Some little thing with a lot of teeth comes along and bites one of them on the ass, and it takes a goddamn week before he even notices. By the time he turns around, he's had his ass bit right off. That's why they died out."

Bannister nodded thoughtfully, trying to imagine how dinosaurs would go about making baby dinosaurs.

"Now, you take any kind of organization," Al continued. "A government, or a company, or any goddamn thing. When it starts off it's out there rooting around and getting things done, right? It's competing, right? If it's successful, it gets bigger. The more successful it is, the bigger it gets. And pretty soon it's like one of them goddamn dinosaurs."

"Right," said the other consultant.

"Only," Al said, pointing his fork across the table, "only, smart organizations don't die out. No matter how big they get. And you wanna know why?" He put down his fork and leaned forward over his plate.

"Look at it this way. That dinosaur I was talking about, what did he need? He needed to know that little thing with all the teeth was coming ·before it got anywheres near him. You know what that is? Information. Intelligence. And he needed to smack it down and stomp on it before it got close enough to bite him on the ass. You know what that is? Security." Al leaned back and folded his arms.

"That's what it's all about. Security and Intelligence. Any big organization, if it's going to stay alive, it's got to have something that'll short-cut all them proper channels and organization charts and get the job done. That's why Napoleon had his secret service. That's why the goddamn Russkies got the KGB."

"That's why we've got the CIA," the other consultant added.

Al eyed him disapprovingly. "Yeah," he said. "Only those guys have become a dinosaur themselves. But that's another story. Listen, Bronco— that's what they call you, right?— you want another cup of coffee?"

There had been more lunches and more rambling lectures in which many of the themes from the first were repeated. Gradually, Bannister had become aware of a world beyond the drill rigs and production platforms that had so far occupied most of his attention. Al's vivid metaphors made it a jungle world where corporate and governmental giants thrashed and heaved, sometimes in ponderous competition, and sometimes in lumbering cooperation. In the shadows of the undergrowth smaller, faster creatures darted, dealing in the two commodities that the giants needed to stay alive: Intelligence and Security.

Eventually, Bannister had been offered a job in the undergrowth. Over the past eighteen of his forty-eight years he had been on the payroll of one or another of a score of companies in as many different countries. He had been salesman, consultant, engineer, caterer, roustabout, or drilling supervisor as occasion required, not always under his own name. But wherever he went and whatever he did, his instructions came always from the same place: a firm of petroleum industry consultants based in Houston, Texas, not all that far from the farm— or ranch— of his birth. He did not know the exact structure of this organization; one of the things that made him a good field man was a discreet lack of curiosity about matters that did not concern the job in hand.

His organization's relations with Pastor Jarvis's employers were rather like those between a large private security firm and a police force: a professional rivalry in which, although most of the time they were on the same side, each felt that the other did not fully appreciate the significance of things, and each took delight in showing the other up when opportunity arose.

Currently, Bannister was the newly appointed Managing Director of a recently incorporated oil and gas industry consulting firm called Hibernian International Petro-industry Expediters (Canada) Ltd. The exact corporate structure of the company was not Bannister's concern. Government regulations required that companies engaged in providing service to the oil industry in Newfoundland be fifty per cent locally-owned, and so presumably HIPE (Canada) was, but just how the names on the articles of incorporation came to be there was not easy to determine.

Anyway, Bannister wasted no time thinking along that line. He knew his business. Oil companies exploring on the Grand Banks would give contracts to HIPE (Canada) for economic surveys, environmental impact assessments, and later for on-shore site management tasks, and Bannister would hire specialists and grant sub-contracts and get the jobs done. Meanwhile, he would be responsible to Al and the Houston office for seeing that things happened the way they should.

It was not the first time he had done such a job, which made his little fumble at the beginning all the more irritating. However, he was too much of a professional to waste energy worrying over it, and he quickly swung, with the ease of long practice, into a set of procedures that he had once summarized for a younger colleague: "Get a fancy office, hire an old battle-axe to run it and a couple of young popsies for decoration, then find out who's got what you need and go get it."

Bannister did not have to spend very long interviewing Miss Hiscock before he knew she was just what he wanted for the position of office manager.

"Marge," he said, "I think you and me are going to be able to do business. I feel real good about it."

Miss Hiscock's feelings on the matter were much more mixed. To be interviewed for a job at all was traumatic, but to be interviewed by a man who sat with his decorated cowboy boots propped on the desk, and chewed gum and scraped at his fingernails with a pocket-knife while he asked her questions, was almost more than she could bear. She was also not quite sure how to respond to his last remark.

"Yes," she said. "Just what sort of business is... ah...Hibernian International...?"

"HIPE," Bannister cut in. "I just call it HIPE. Hell of a name, either way. It's consulting. It'll be just you and me and a steno or two at first. We'll hire on specialists as we need them. Could get pretty big after a while, but there'll be plenty of room; I've taken an option on this whole floor. From what you've told me about your last job, why, this one will be right up your alley." Miss Hiscock was not so sure. However, the suite of offices that was taking shape around them as they talked looked impressive, and in any case she was in no position to be choosy. This was only the second time she had applied for a job in a working career of nearly forty years.

Miss Hiscock's background could hardly have been more different from Bannister's if they had belonged to different species. She had been born, inconveniently, at a time when her parents had long since accepted the idea that they would have no children and had reached a stage of life when the last possibility of it seemed past. Her father, a minor civil servant in His Majesty's Government of Newfoundland, had no resources but his meagre salary on which to accomplish what became his life's over-riding purpose— to bring up his unexpected daughter in a manner befitting a member of the St. John's middle class.

Through the bleak years of the Depression he managed so successfully to provide her with the proper clothes and send her to the right schools that he earned among his colleagues a reputation for having devised some completely original system of embezzlement. Long after his death, civil servants were still hoping to find out what it was and get in on it, but their hopes were in vain. There was no system: he did it all through superhuman efforts of domestic economy and self-denial. The spartan regime was too much for Miss Hiscock's mother, who faded away shortly after her birth.

During the Second World War, while girls not much older than she was were compromising themselves with American servicemen on Water Street, Miss Hiscock was learning elocution and deportment at Bishop Spencer Academy. After the War, both her accent and her attitudes were given a final polish at a school for would-be young ladies in England, financed by the sale of her father's modest house on the less-fashionable end of Circular Road. She returned to a changed world, a Canadian citizen by an Act of Parliament and an orphan by an act, presumably, of God; Newfoundland had become the tenth province of Canada, and her father had finally exhausted his resources.

The timing of his death, though he could hardly know it, solved a problem that had been bothering him for some time— the question of what she was to do on her return from England. With a frugal practicality that would have made him proud, she invested the tiny legacy from his life insurance policy in some secretarial training and approached one of his old school friends who, for old time's sake, gave her a job in the small contracting business he had established on the strength of his close relations with the now-reigning Liberal Party.

Like many another company of the right political bent, her employer's business grew and flourished in the manner of the green bay tree of the Biblical story, expanding into half a dozen other fields. In what seemed in retrospect a very short time, Miss Hiscock found herself entering middle age as the manager of a sizeable office; house-mother to an ever increasing brood of clerks, typists and secretaries of whom she demanded and usually succeeded in getting a level of elocution and deportment which, if not up to Bishop Spencer standards, was still well above the average.

Her job did not require her to know just how the government contracts that made up most of the business were arranged, which was probably just as well. It also did not require her to know anything about the activities of her original employer's son, who took over the business when the government changed in 1972 and cultivated the same sort of interest in the newly-reigning Conservative Party as his father had in the Liberals.

Even less did it require her to know anything of the curious personal habits the young man developed in the decade or so after his father's retirement to Florida. It came as a distinct surprise, therefore, when she arrived at work one morning— early, as usual— not long after her fifty-ninth birthday, to find bailiffs and policemen wreaking havoc among the files, and business suspended pending investigations of interest not only to the Royal Newfoundland Constabulary and the Royal Canadian Mounted Police, but to several foreign police agencies as well.

For the first time in her life, Miss Hiscock was out of a job.

The company had carried its own pension plan, but as nearly as anyone could determine its funds had been invested in a boat which had been seized after an unscheduled voyage from somewhere in Colombia. The money was tied up, in both the legal and the nautical senses of the term, in Panama.

Miss Hiscock had inherited her father's respect for appearances: she dressed well and lived in respectable comfort. As a consequence, she had very little money in the bank. After a lifetime of railing against layabouts and ne'er-do-wells, she was subjected to the ignominy of drawing Unemployment Insurance, a humiliation compounded beyond measure when she was told at the Employment Canada office by a chit of a girl with bad posture and a whining, nasal voice that she was far too old to expect to find another job.

Bannister, of course, could know nothing of most of this. All he knew was that he had in front of him the very prototype of the "old battle-axe" of his maxim: a woman who could set up his office and run it, no matter how big the staff might get, leaving him to get on with his real work. And, as a bonus, a woman of consider-able experience who knew something—but not too much—about what went on in every office, governmental or private, from St. John's to Port aux Basques.

He did not want to lose her. He acted casual, and called her by her first name to put her at her ease.

"Marge," he said, "I think we can make a deal. Now, the salary that was mentioned in the ad, when I settled on that I wasn't thinking about somebody with your kind of experience. I think we can bump that up by a thousand or so. What do you say?"

Miss Hiscock looked at the soles of his cowboy boots facing her over the desk and searched unsuccessfully for a tactful way to let him know that no one had ever before called her Marge for a second time. Then she thought of the adenoidal little employment officer and the dwindling number of weeks left in her Unemployment claim.

"Very well, Mr. Bannister. I think that will be satisfactory. When would you like me to begin?"

Miss Hiscock took over interviewing applicants for the one stenographer/clerk who was to be hired to start off. Bannister, with his established procedures in mind, interviewed them too.

Among the candidates was Theresa Foley, whose brief background was nothing like that of either of her prospective bosses. She had been born in the tiny hamlet of St. Kevin's, attended elementary school at St. Cyril's and secondary at Holy Rosary Regional High School for Girls, where her prematurely burgeoning charms made her classmates grit their teeth in envy and the teaching sisters pray that she would achieve a decent Christian marriage without undue delay.

A stenographic course at the College of Trades and Technology completed her formal education. Her real education, of course, came from television, movies, supermarket tabloids, and Harlequin romances. These provided her with, among other things, the inspiration for the clothing and make-up in which she presented herself at the HIPE (Canada) offices for her first job interview.

Miss Hiscock rejected her out of hand because of her appearance and deportment. Bronco Bannister over-ruled Miss Hiscock and hired her for exactly the same reasons— for those, but primarily for one other, the existence of which neither Theresa nor Miss Hiscock could possibly suspect.

Miss Hiscock, certainly, didn't suspect it, but she did recognize the half-nostalgic, half-predatory gleam in his eye when he announced his decision, and took note of the Freudian implications when he observed that Theresa would "round out" the staff nicely for now. She tightened her lips, said "Very well" in a pointed sort of way, and filed the names of the other applicants for future reference.

HIPE (Canada) was in business.

IV

Miss Hiscock, with Theresa at least nominally under her direction, took over the job of completing the furnishing and decoration of the offices, and each of them undertook the private project of shaping the other's behaviour into something more to her liking.

Perhaps it would be more correct to say that Miss Hiscock set out to convert the unpromising material of Theresa into something closer to her notion of a proper office employee. Theresa, for her part, gave the matter no thought at all, but merely reacted with the passive resistance and subliminal insolence that evolution, over countless generations, has made instinctive among schoolgirls dealing with tough old nuns.

Bannister was vaguely aware of the undercurrents but paid them no attention as he went about his double job of getting HIPE (Canada) started in the consulting business and learning his way around so that he could perform his other, less public, function. He reported regularly to Al by telephone, and although he had to put up with occasional caustic reminders of his first day in St. John's, they were soon back on sufficiently cordial terms that he could indulge himself from time to time in complaint.

"It's a funny place, Al. You know, in most places it's the natives that give you trouble— or the Russkies or somebody. Here, most of the problems I've got are with goddamn Gringos, hundred per cent Americans."

"Like that spook preacher, for instance?"

"Yeah. Him for instance number one. He is one big pain in the ass, let me tell you."

"When did you ever know a CIA guy who *wasn't* a pain in the ass?"

"Okay. Granted. But not like this one. Most of them kind of fade into the background, but this guy.... Why couldn't he have some other kind of cover, for God's sake, like a salesman or a trade commissioner or something? He acts like I'm some kind of charter member of his crummy church. Barges into my office two or three times a week hollering 'God bless you' all over the place. Its downright embarrassing, Al."

"A bit of religion might do you good, Bronco."

"I'd rather deal with a goddamn Ayatollah. What bugs me is the way this guy kind of pretends he knows everything about what I'm doing. I don't know how much he knows or even why he bothers."

"He's a bird-dog, old buddy. If he can find a way to make you look bad, he'll look good. You know how those guys operate. So what other Gringos are giving you a hard time?"

"Well, there's this Schultz...."

"The P.R. guy for Mogul Oil?"

"Yeah. Only now they call it Community Liaison. Another pain in the ass. Listen Al, what do we know about him?"

"Nothing you haven't got. He's been around there a while. Went to university there or something. Mogul seems to think he's a hotshot on local knowledge."

"So does he. Listen, we were supposed to get a few contracts from Mogul so we could get this operation off the ground, right? Only trouble is, for some reason this Schultz guy has to approve them. And instead of approving them he's screwing around asking me all kinds of questions. Could he be spooking for somebody, do you think?"

"Like who?"

"How the hell should I know? Like MIA. Or DIA. Or one of the other oil outfits. Maybe even Mogul itself. All I know is, he's awful goddamn nosy for a straight citizen. Listen, if he's Mogul's spook and they ain't telling us, I'm going to be goddamn good and mad."

"Take it easy, Bronco. It's their show. They pay the bills, we do our job. If they want somebody looking over your shoulder, it's their business."

"Well, with him on one side and Jarvis on the other, I got no shoulders left. I hate this place. When this is over I got some holidays coming...."

"Why, Bronco, that whole job's a holiday. People pay big money for a peaceful few months by the ocean. Tell me, how's your office staff? How are you doing with that little chickie you were telling me about?"

"You know me, Al. Bronco does all right. Now, anybody looking over my shoulder in that department might really learn something. Listen, dig around and see if you can find out anything about Schultz, will you?"

Al's digging brought nothing new to light. Brad Schultz was one of the wave of young Americans who arrived in Canada in the late 1960s, some disgusted by their own country's excesses in Southeast Asia, and some just seeking greener fields.

He turned up as a graduate student in Political Science at Memorial University of Newfoundland, bringing with him a heady whiff of New Left politics, resistance to the Viet Nam war, civil rights demonstrations, and Acapulco Gold. He took part in a few sit-ins in the university president's office and protests in front of the American Consulate, got himself elected to several student organizations, and quickly learned how to get grant money out of the Department of the Secretary of State.

Upon graduation, he trimmed his hair and beard, gave up his khaki knapsack, took to wearing a shirt and tie, and landed a job with the provincial Department of Rural Revitalization. Along the way he managed, over considerable resistance from her family, to marry one of the younger and more impressionable daughters of the St. John's mercantile aristocracy.

In the mid-1970s, when exploratory drilling for oil and gas on the Grand Banks began to show results, there was a flurry of public interest in the possible effects of offshore petroleum development. Delegations of civil servants, task forces of politicians, film crews, and university professors on research grants shuttled back and forth between the North Sea oil fields and St. John's, bringing back reports of house prices in Aberdeen, psychiatric disorders in Oslo, and oil-fouled sheep in the Shetland Islands.

"WILL ST. JOHN'S BE ANOTHER CALGARY?" the headlines screamed, and the public turned to their government and the oil companies, some seeking confirmation of their hopes that it would, and others desperate for reassurance that it would not. Mogul Oil, a major player in the field, advertised for a Community Liaison Officer. Brad Schultz applied, and got the job.

The appointment occasioned some mild surprise, especially among the handful of his professors who had read his Master's thesis on the inherent immorality of multinational corporations. Mogul Oil, however, was delighted.

Their new employee was an American, which reassured them, but a Landed Immigrant in Canada, which made him easy to hire. He knew his way around Newfoundland, and the faint, lingering aura of radicalism that still clung to him gave their efforts to deal with the public a nice ring of sincerity.

Thus it was that Brad Schultz became one of the key people in deciding upon the bread-and-butter consulting contracts that would go to HIPE (Canada) to provide cover for Bannister's activities. As the resident expert on explaining Mogul Oil to the citizenry and explaining Newfoundland to Mogul Oil, Schultz kept a close eye on anything that might impinge on his area of expertise— and thus he joined the list of Gringos getting in Bannister's way.

Shortly after his conversation with Al checking up on Schultz, Bannister was sitting in his office flicking rolled-up bits of paper at the wastebasket when the intercom buzzed and Miss Hiscock announced that Schultz himself was in the outer office. Bannister could hear him in the background, breezily chatting with Theresa. He snarled silently, lofted a final ball of paper, and told Miss Hiscock to send him in.

Schultz entered, looked around with an irritatingly proprietorial air, and sank uninvited into a soft chair by the coffee table in the corner of the room. "Hey, Bronco," he said. "How you doin'? Your place is looking real nice."

"Yeah," said Bannister. "It's okay."

It was his custom, when visitors came, to call out to Miss Hiscock for coffee. The first time he had done it she sent Theresa in, but he informed her that he wanted her to do it herself. He felt that having what he thought of as "an old broad— like somebody's mother" serving coffee to his guests created a nice, hospitable atmosphere.

He had not noticed that it also created a violent but suppressed crisis in the outer office each time it occurred. Miss Hiscock flushed and clenched her teeth, Theresa smirked and looked knowing. Only the image of the unemployment office prevented Miss Hiscock from pouring the coffee over Bannister's head.

This time he didn't call, and Miss Hiscock, who had been flushing in anticipation, relaxed. Theresa yawned and looked disappointed.

"It's okay," Bannister repeated, not getting up. "We could use a few contracts, though, if we're going to stay in business. I thought you guys were supposed to have lots of work for us."

Schultz ignored the suggestion. "Nice little bit of stuff on the reception desk," he said. Bannister didn't answer. "I guess your girls haven't got much to do yet?"

With some effort, Bannister continued to remain silent. Schultz put his feet up on the coffee table. "We've got a few contracts coming up that would suit you. I just want to look them over first. In the meantime, though, there's a little job you could help out with."

"Yeah?" said Bannister. "What?"

"It's nothing much. Just a bit of routine paperwork. It would give your girls something to do and it would help us out."

Bannister grunted noncommittally.

"You know we've got this community liaison programme going? We send out these information kits to people in an area, then we follow it up with a big community meeting. 'What Offshore Oil Development Means To You,' we call it. Some of us go out and tell the locals all about all the jobs they're going to get, only not to get too excited because they're not going to get them yet, and stuff like that."

"P.R.," said Bannister.

"Community Liaison. We're big on controlled development. Mogul Oil, Responsible Corporate Citizen, that's us. Anyway, right now we've got a batch of these information kits to go out, and our office is real busy. Your girls could do the job in— oh, a day or so. We've got all the addresses on computer— all your people have to do is put the kits together, stuff the envelopes, stick on the labels...."

"So hire somebody. Don't tell me Mogul's short of money."

Schultz slipped easily into the role of Resident Expert. "In a place like this, with unemployment and all, it's better not to hire people for temporary work and lay them off. It creates expectations, and at the same time detracts from the image of permanence and solidity we try to project."

Bannister was feeling decidedly uncooperative. "I'll think about it. I'll let you know."

"We have to get this mailing out. The date for the community meeting is set. It would help us out a lot." Schultz glanced shrewdly across at Bannister. "If I didn't have this to worry about, maybe I could get time to look over those contracts...."

"Where's this P.R. operation going?"

"Community Liaison. It's in an area they call the Hard Shore."

Bannister was suddenly sharply alert, but he kept his voice casual. "Yeah, I've heard of it," he said. Then, after a moment, "Why there?"

"No special reason. We set up a series of these things, covering different areas that might be impacted by offshore development in different ways. It's their turn, is all."

Bannister's blood pressure was rising steadily, but he gave no outward sign. "Yeah," he said. "Well, listen, I've got a couple of things I need to do right now. Then I'll talk to Marge— see if we can handle it. I'll let you know later."

Schultz got up, looking mildly offended. "It's no big deal," he said. "Just a few envelopes...."

"Sure," Bannister said, ushering him to the door. "Right. I'll see what I can do. I'll get back to you."

With Schultz gone, Bannister told Miss Hiscock that he was not to be disturbed, got out his scrambler, and put in a call to Houston. Al was in a meeting, and would call back. Bannister chewed a paper clip, and thought about taking up smoking again.

When he had told Schultz that he had "heard of" the area called the Hard Shore, it was no more than a fraction of the truth. He was, in fact, far more interested in it and, having spent a lot of effort studying the documents he had brought from Houston, knew far more about it than most of the people who lived there. So did a lot of other people in places higher and more powerful than his own, and it was because of this interest that they had sent Bronco Bannister to masquerade as the manager of HIPE (Canada) in St. John's.

It was also because of this interest that Bannister had insisted, over Miss Hiscock's opposition, on hiring Theresa. He would have been tempted, anyway, after having a look at her, but the fact that she had been born and brought up on the Hard Shore clinched it. Bannister never missed an opportunity to make contact with convenient sources of information. It was this sort of attention to detail that made him a good field man.

While the drill rigs ground their way into the ocean floor on the Grand Banks, a lot of planning and a lot of maneuvering was going on in widely-separated and far-off places. Federal and provincial authorities argued over jurisdiction. Oil company executives patiently explained that the technology to be used in exploiting the resource depended on conditions in the oil field, and that the location and type of developments on shore would depend on the technology, and that therefore the impact of such development could not be predicted in any detail. And while all this was happening, technologies were being decided on and plans were being laid.

For public consumption, a variety of possibilities were put forward and discussed in the press. There might be a service centre here, a storage facility there. Several areas were designated by the government as possible development sites. Chambers of Commerce and town councils panted in anticipation.

All the while, in private offices in tall buildings in New York and Houston and Calgary, the real plans took shape. When the time was ripe, a selected stretch of Newfoundland coast would blossom with rig-building sites, pipe-storage yards, loading docks, breakwaters, and catering services on a scale and at a speed beyond anything that local imagination could conceive.

Vast platforms would be built, or brought from somewhere else and serviced. Villages of a few hundred people would be engulfed by sprawling encampments of tough, young, male foreigners. Mountains of concrete, wood, steel, sirloin steak, and artificially flavoured lemon pie would be consumed.

Scores of companies, large and small, would compete for contracts and give each other credit. Some people would make fortunes, more would go bankrupt, and a few of the cleverest would do both at the same time. Politicians would undergo miraculous changes of perspective and make down-payments on condominiums in Florida. Charitable organizations, such as those for unmarried mothers, would receive unexpectedly large donations, and find that they needed every penny.

It was Bannister's task to see that all this happened according to plan.

It was his experience, and the experience of his employers, that there was no stretch of territory in the world so unappetizing, and no collection of people so squalid that somebody, somewhere, would not want to interfere with their sensible development. If there were not guerillas in the hills with rifles, there would be environmentalists in the street with placards, or politicians with inflated ideas about the price of their votes, or labour leaders out to settle a grudge. The juggernaut of massive development, for all its weight and power, could sometimes be halted by surprisingly small obstacles. Someone like Bannister was needed to work quietly and inconspicuously at clearing them away.

In the early stages he would survey the field, identifying potential trouble spots. He would find out what local authorities needed to be placated, what tribal leaders needed to be pacified. He would ensure that key sites were held by owners who could be depended upon. As work began, he would deal with problems as they arose. If a strike were to threaten the progress of the plan, he would arrange for it to be settled or broken. If a strike were needed to slow down some aspect, he would see that one took place.

By the time the oil began to flow, Bronco Bannister would have a network of operatives with backgrounds rather like those of the Reverend Mr. Jarvis's assistants, established in key positions as engineers or economists or technicians, ready for someone else to take over, and he would be ready for a well-deserved rest. All this was what Bannister had been sent to Newfoundland to do.

And he was to do it on the Hard Shore.

"Al," he said, when his call finally came through from Houston, "Al, I cannot believe that this is happening."

"Don't tell me it's snowing again, Bronco. I couldn't handle it."

"Al, this is serious." He explained at some length. "...Now, do you believe that? He's going to go and do a big P.R. job, all about offshore oil and development, right smack in the middle of the Target Area! My God, he'll have them so fired up I won't be able to move for a year. And he wants my staff to...." Bannister broke off in incoherent noises.

"God, Bronco, I don't know. It does sound crazy to me, I got to admit. I can't believe he's planning all that and Mogul doesn't know about it. I mean, maybe their local bunch don't know anything about the Target Area yet. They're mostly exploration types— they don't need to know. But, my God, I just can't believe that the guys who set up the plan aren't keeping an eye on all this Community Liaison stuff. They must know what he's doing!"

"It doesn't make any sense. What the hell do they want us in there for if they're going to let him screw us up like this? What the hell are they up to?"

"Bronco, I will do what I can. I will make inquiries. I will shake Mogul's ass. I'll get back to you."

When Al called back, he delivered no consolation. "It's crazy, Bronco, but there it is. They know what's going on, and they say to let him alone. Correction, they say to give him full cooperation. This Schultz guy must be pretty good. He's got the Mogul brass believing he's the only one who knows anything about that God-forsaken place. So tough it out, Bronco, old buddy. As I keep telling you, it's their show. They're paying the bills, and they call the shots."

"Yeah," said Bannister. "And what happens when it all gets screwed up? You think they're going to say, 'Oh, sorry. We made a mistake.'? You know goddamn well who's going to take all the shit. Us. Or, more precisely, me."

He was still fuming when Schultz returned that afternoon and took possession of the soft chair by the coffee table.

"My, my," Schultz said. "You've been a busy boy, Bronco. Calls going back and forth to Houston. Wires burning up. You people shouldn't be so excitable."

"So you know about that?"

"I know about it. Mogul trusts me, Bronco. I'm their resident local expert, remember?"

"What else do you know?"

"I know what you're here for. I know about the Target Area. The Big Brass have taken me into their confidence. They want me to work closely with you—give you the benefit of my vast knowledge." Bannister drew in his breath, searching for some scathing retort, but Schultz cut him off.

"...So just take it easy, Bronco. Your secret is safe with me, as they say on the Late Show."

Bannister let out the breath in a long sigh. "Okay," he said. "So if you know about the Target Area, what are you going to do about this P.R. scheme?"

"Community Liaison," said Schultz blandly. "I'm going ahead with it, of course. If you'd give me a chance to explain, you'd understand...."

"I understand one thing," Bannister snapped. "I understand that in this business you point in one direction and you jump in another. You don't go making trouble for yourself. I also understand that goddamn amateurs...."

"Look, Bannister," Schultz said, "that community meeting is going ahead on the Hard Shore. The information kits are going out whether your girls send them or not. I decide on what goes where in the Community Liaison programme. You can cooperate or you can sulk, just as you choose. But I'd advise you to cooperate. Your boss already checked with Mogul, didn't he? What did he tell you?"

Bannister gritted his teeth. "So while I'm supposed to be doing the groundwork, you're going to be in there making sure the natives get all fired up about oil development. Great. Brilliant. Only, if Mogul wants to screw up the whole project, why the hell didn't they ask me? I could screw it up for them myself, and save all this hassle. Like, maybe I could hire a sound truck and drive around telling everybody...."

Schultz held up his hand. "Bronco, if we're going to work together, you're going to have to learn from old Brad. I understand the psychology of this thing. Anyway, everybody knows The Shore is a potential development area. There's already a lot of rumours and speculation going on. It's inevitable."

"Okay. But what kind of sense does it make to go holding a big meeting to get them fired up even more?"

"That's the psychology part. Once that meeting is held—hell, once it's even announced—they're going to be convinced the development's going some place else."

Bannister's jaw dropped. "You can't go telling them something like that!" he said, horrified. "You could never get away with that! The fundamental rule of this business...."

"Funny," said Schultz. "I always thought you undercover guys were unflappable. You know— steely-eyed, calm, all that kind of stuff. You had your blood-pressure checked lately? You look kind of red in the face."

"That's because we usually only have to deal with Russians and Ay-rab terrorists," Bannister said bitterly. "Mostly we ain't used to being jacked around by our own people."

"If you'd just hold still and listen, Bronco, you'd feel better. I have no intention of telling those people on The Shore anything that's going to embarrass Mogul later on. I'm going to do the standard Community Liaison package, 'What Oil Development Means to You.' How different kinds of technology means different kinds of onshore development, what kinds of jobs are created, etcetera, etcetera."

"And that's not going to get them thinking they're the Target Area?"

"Exactly the opposite," said Schultz with an exaggerated show of patience. "I tell you, you've got to understand the psychology of it. And the history. For the past hundred years Newfoundlanders have been expecting something big to happen to them. Development. Big money. Governments have been promising it at every election.

"A hundred years ago it was the railway. Then it was pulp and paper. Then it was mines or hydro development, or factories. Now it's offshore oil."

"Yeah?" Bannister said. "Seems to me that just makes the job tougher. Them Ay-rabs, now, they never expected anything. It took them years to...."

"Never mind the Arabs. This is Newfoundland. Okay, so they never got the big bonanza their government kept telling them was just around the corner. But they did get something. The railway got built, for instance. They had to give away half the damn country to do it, but the railway got built. The hydro got developed. They had to give the power away to Quebec and a couple of big companies, but it got developed. People got jobs for a while. There was some action."

"We're going around in circles, here," Bannister said. "I don't see...."

"Stick with me, Bronco," Schultz said. "You're in good hands. I've given lectures on this stuff."

"Yes, I bet you have," said Bannister.

"Okay, so that's the pattern. Big development always just ahead, and in the meantime, some little stuff going on here and there. For the past thirty-five years or so, since they joined Canada, governments have been feeding the pattern. They keep up the promises, and they deal out a bit of construction here, build a road there, do a pilot project, an exploratory study, whatever. The pilot projects don't pan out, the exploratory studies need more exploration. Unemployment stays high and gets higher, but there's always a bit of action. A bit of movement."

"I'm sure it's a great lecture," Bannister said. "It must knock 'em dead in Mogul's home office. But what I want to know is...."

"Patience, Bronco, patience. We're getting close to the end. The result of all this is that people get cynical as hell. They don't really believe in prosperity just around the corner any more, but when things are always tough, and there aren't enough jobs, and everything costs more than it did last year well, you want to believe in *something*. So they believe in the big bonanza the way they believe in the lotteries. You don't really expect to win, but still, you never know. See what I mean?"

"Is this leading some place?" Bannister said. "As far as I can see, you're still planning to screw up my work."

Schultz ignored him. "They know the government deals out these little bits of action— a slip-way, a wharf, a bit of pavement— a few jobs and a bit of money. Every little piss-pot community wants their share, and somebody else's if they can get it. They keep bugging the government. It's a way of life, man."

"I keep listening, Schultz, but I still can't see what this has to do with our situation."

"It has everything to do with it. See, every once in awhile, some area gets the idea that they want some real development. Something that will give more or less permanent jobs, or something big that will at least give a lot of them. They start leaning on the government a bit extra.

"So the government worked out how to deal with that. Whenever there was some extra pressure from some area, the government would hold a big development conference. Go out and tell them how great it is that they've got all this ambition. Talk to them about long-term planning. Benefits down the road, all that. I've been here—Jesus, twenty years, man—I've seen it all. I used to go to those things. Hell, when I was with the government I used to plan them."

"So?"

"So whenever an area gets one of these development conferences, they know damn well they're not going to get any factories or oil refineries or fish plants in the foreseeable future.

"That's why," Schultz said with a touch of pride, "I modelled these Community Liaison meetings of mine on the development conferences."

Bannister, finally, was becoming interested in spite of himself. "What I don't see," he said, "is why people don't get mad. I mean, if they really know that they're not going to get what they want?"

"That's the neat part," Schultz said. "Remember what I said about the lottery. They don't really expect to get a big prize, but they try anyway, just in case. On the other hand, they know that if they can push the government hard enough to get them to hold a development conference, then the government's going to have to come through with something. Like a consolation prize, you might say.

"I'm telling you, Bronco," he concluded, "that's the way it works. Any place that gets one of those development conferences, the people know damn well they're not going to get any big stuff, but they figure they're going to get some sort of little spin-off. That's all they figured they'd get anyhow, so they're happy. More or less. Quiet for a while, anyway.

"So that's the whole psychology of these Community Liaison meetings. I designed them to be as much like the government ones as I could make them without getting sued for plagiarism. I guarantee you, if we hold that meeting on The Shore, as per my schedule, it'll make your job ten times easier. Now, aren't you sorry about all those nasty things you said?"

"I don't know," Bannister grumbled. "It still seems pretty dumb to me. I never heard of barging into a target area that way."

"There's lot's of things around here you've never heard of, Bronco. Trust me. I'll send the stuff around tomorrow morning and come by and show your girls what to do, okay?"

"Well...," Bannister said.

"Great. See you in the morning."

Schultz called cheery farewells to Theresa and Miss Hiscock as he left.

V

Schultz was at the HIPE (Canada) offices early next morning with a deliveryman carrying boxes of paper. In annoying detail he showed Miss Hiscock and Theresa how to assemble the information packages.

"We've got all the names in the computer," he said. "I've had it crank out the address labels randomly. That way they won't arrive in any one community ahead of any other. You got to be careful about little things like that. These people can get real jealous of each other."

Theresa was not interested in the niceties of community liaison, but she was fascinated by the project. The Shore was her home, after all, and she knew a great many of the people whose names appeared on the labels. Already she was thinking of ways to avoid Miss Hiscock's sharp eye and slip personal notes into the packets addressed to favoured uncles, aunts, and cousins. She smiled charmingly at Schultz, wishing he would go away and let her get on with it.

Miss Hiscock was ambivalent. It pleased her to have some actual work going on in the office at last. She had for several days been hard pressed to find enough to occupy her own and Theresa's time. On the other hand, she was not at all happy at the thought of doing such a routine job herself, on the same footing as a little clerk just out of Trades College. She repeated each of Schultz's instructions to Theresa, as though translating for a particulary dim-witted foreigner. Finally Schultz breezed out, promising to drop by later to see how the job was going. Both women smiled and hoped he wouldn't.

Bannister left, too, to make the rounds of oil-related agencies, picking up bits of information, introducing himself where he was not already known, making contacts. It was the sort of thing he usually enjoyed, but on this day his heart was not in it. The thought of what his employees were doing preyed on his mind, and he drifted back to HIPE (Canada) after lunch. Miss Hiscock and Theresa were working steadily in strained silence. He retired to his inner office, leaving strict instructions that he was not to be disturbed.

He was tempted to put his feet up on the desk and brood, but shook off the feeling and took from a desk drawer a compact strongbox sealed with an inconspicuous but elaborate array of combination locks. He opened it gingerly. It was also fitted with a device that would incinerate the contents if there were any attempt to force it, and he had heard stories of such things going off by accident. The way his luck was running, he could just imagine the damn thing blowing up in his face.

Inside, in sheaves of paper and packets of microfiche, was the accumulated product of thousands of hours of painstaking work by dozens of skilled specialists: satellite photographs, demographic tables, socio-economic analyses, large-scale contour maps and shoreline charts, adding up to an astonishingly complete and detailed picture of his Target Area. With the contents of this small box he could plot, if need be, the location of the last length of pipe in the latest sewer system of the smallest hamlet on the Hard Shore to possess one, and do it with greater accuracy than the Public Works crews who might wish to dig it up for repairs, as they frequently did.

Bannister slipped a card marked "History" into the microfilm reader on his desk and flicked through it idly. For all that he appreciated close attention to detail he found himself wishing, not for the first time, that the research department would exercise a little restraint. Why, for example, would they include copies of correspondence from the *Gentlemen's Magazine* for 1873-74 on the subject of how his Target Area got its name?

In spite of his irritation, though, he found himself reading an excerpt from a ponderously playful article by a Mr. Cleophas Bootle, B.D., of Bottomley, Herts., on the amusing place-names he had encountered during a tour of duty in Newfoundland. "'The Hard Shore' seems a curious appellation," Mr. Bootle wrote, "for what appears to be a stretch of coastline no more, though certainly no less, forbidding than any other of that rocky isle. However, the fact that it is occupied by fractious Irish fisherfolk of the Romish persuasion renders the name peculiarly apposite from the point of view of a representative of the Established Church."

This was followed by a letter from a Professor McKeirahan, of Cork, suggesting that name was almost certainly a corruption of the Irish *ard seorbh*, meaning "extremely unpleasant" or "intolerable." Since the parents and grandparents of the Irish fisherfolk to whom the Reverend Mr. Bootle had referred had gone there initially in the capacity of indentured servants, little better than slaves to the English fish merchants, it would not be surprising, Professor McKeirahan felt, if they should refer with bitterness to their place of exile.

The correspondence ended with a submission from Admiral Sir Alexander Capstick, R.N.(Ret.), who observed that whether it was originally English, Irish or Chinese, the name was entirely accurate as far as he was concerned. The remainder of his letter consisted of a lengthy memoir of having been wrecked there sixty years earlier, when he was a midshipman in the *Thalia*, during the war with the Americans.

His mood somewhat improved by this excursion into the nineteenth century, Bannister put the microfiche back in the box and took out the plain envelope that contained the most sensitive and secret document of all. Here, on thin, crinkly paper that would flash into smoke and ashes at the slightest touch of a spark, closely printed in pale brownish type that was supposed to resist being copied or photographed, was the product for which all the rest of the information had been so carefully put together: the Master Plan for the development of the Target Area.

Packed into its fifty-odd pages was all the information for which politicians and speculators would gleefully have bartered any portion of their souls that remained un-mortgaged: a step-by-step account of the coming events that would transform the barren coves of the Hard Shore— for a time, at least— into one of the largest industrial sites in the western world.

Bannister flipped through to a section where a series of terse outlines, inevitably called "scenarios," anticipated a variety of political crises and their resolution. His mood darkened again. He could recognize the CIA's hand here— the typical effort to inflate their own importance by what they called "preparing for all eventualities." Even Bannister, who had experienced some pretty difficult eventualities in his career, was alarmed by what they had seen fit to include. The fact that their wild speculations made such documents ten times more sensitive than they needed to be never seemed to deter them.

But even those crazy bastards, he told himself disgustedly, couldn't have thought up this one— Bronco Bannister's staff helping to set up a big public meeting on oil development in the middle of the Target Area.

Well, there was nothing more he could do about that. With an effort, he turned his mind to the task that made up the major part of this stage of his work— the meticulous piecing together of tiny and apparently useless bits of information.

He had hired Theresa because she had grown up on The Hard Shore and he had intended to use her, through casual conversations over a long period of time, as a source of scraps of detail that might come in handy later on. Since she was now involved in stuffing envelopes addressed to the area, at least he could start the process without having to edge into it. He strolled through to the main office and asked how the job was going with the bluff heartiness that he had adopted as his public persona.

Theresa responded with alarm and confusion. She had not, so far, had much directly to do with her employer, and he was for her still a somewhat remote and rather frightening figure. He had, however, played a prominent role in certain aspects of her fantasy life.

Since in spite of Miss Hiscock's best efforts Theresa had not had a great deal of real work to do as yet, she had fallen into the practice of diverting herself, whenever Miss Hiscock was out of earshot, with the telephone. Girls she had known at school and at the Trades College were scattered in offices around the city, in jobs similar to her own, doing menial tasks for the minimum wage and fated to be laid off as soon as they came close to qualifying for a higher rate of pay.

Together, they had developed a telephone network that any intelligence agency would envy, complete with codes for letting each other know when they could not talk freely, where they might meet at lunch-time, and other such momentous matters. When two of them could escape detection at the same time, they carried on a continuing, if often interrupted, flow of chat and gossip.

The girls were all very young and in their first jobs, so much of their attention was focused on their bosses and co-workers. The whole point of the thing was mutual entertainment, and since they were the product of a society with a strong oral tradition, their gossip tended to be heavily and imaginatively embroidered.

Theresa was more fortunate than most of them in having good basic material to work with. Miss Hiscock was an excellent subject for caricature, and among the bosses, most of whom were grey and pot-bellied and uninteresting, Bannister provided a nice touch of the exotic.

"He's pretty old," Theresa would tell the members of her network, "but he's sort of distinguished. Like Paul Newman, or somebody. Only taller. He wears these fancy cowboy boots— and you should hear him talk! Just like J.R. on Dallas!" When she had exhausted the topic of his appearance, she went on to hint that in spite of his age and distinction he took more than a passing interest in herself, and that he had indicated that he might well want her to accompany him "as a sort of private secretary, like," to New York or some other romantic destination.

"And I'd go, too," she would add casually, which would elicit, as it was meant to, squeals and giggles and exclamations of disbelief.

Although Bannister was completely unaware of them, Theresa's fantasies in some degree ran parallel to some of his own. Among his colleagues he tried to project a macho image, and in conversations with Houston he had managed to convey that his relations with her were of a very intimate and athletic kind. He tended to exaggerate her age a little: now that Al's daughter by his second marriage had reached the age of seventeen he was no longer amused by stories of adventures with young women under twenty. Otherwise Bannister described Theresa fairly accurately, but in terms that would have horrified her if she could have heard them.

She could not, of course, help noticing that he sometimes looked at her appreciatively, but she was used to such looks from men of all ages and accepted them with the self-centredness of the very young, without thinking too much about what motivated them. From movies, television, and magazines purporting to tell the true stories of girls very much like herself, she was well schooled in the theory of sexual intrigue, but she was almost completely lacking in practical experience, and would have been completely at a loss had she been confronted with any of the scenes she outlined so freely to her friends.

Whenever Bannister addressed her directly, even on the most ordinary of topics, he appeared to her not as the romantic figure of her stories but as a symbol of adult male authority, like a policeman or a priest, and she became almost tongue-tied with shyness. In her confusion, she lost the veneer of office-talk demanded by Miss Hiscock, and lapsed into the more natural speech patterns she used with her friends, with the result that Bannister could not understand most of what she said.

Bannister was also somewhat constrained when he spoke to Theresa. The erotic adventures he described to his colleagues were part of a lurid fiction they all maintained— a sort of grown-up version of high school locker room talk, rooted in thrillers of the James Bond genre, but in real life he had never been able to live up to the image. For one thing, it was professionally dangerous: even casual liaisons had a way of creating difficulties in delicate operations.

The main reason, however, which he found it difficult to admit even to himself, was that he was not very good at it. As a clandestine operative, he was skilled at ingratiating himself, manipulating friendships, causing people to do things they did not really want to do. But somehow he had never been able to make use of these skills in relationships with women. Especially with young women of the sort who were the raw material of the fantasies, he was too fearful of rejection to even know how to begin.

The contrast between the fantasy and the reality left him feeling inadequate and awkward, and he treated Theresa with that bantering, slightly possessive familiarity that middle-aged men usually adopt toward young female employees about whom they sometimes entertain improper thoughts.

With all these undercurrents, their conversation tended to be painfully stilted. Miss Hiscock, for whom after thirty years of office experience the whole thing was tediously familiar, found it intolerable. She stood it as long as she could, while Bannister made ponderous pleasantries and Theresa blushed and giggled and admitted that the job was going "all right" and that, yes, she did indeed come from The Shore, and that she knew a lot of people there, and even that some of them were her very own relatives. When Miss Hiscock could take no more of it, she excused herself and went off to attend to something else.

Bannister was not learning much, but he ploughed on. "I guess you must know this government member from down there," he said. "What we'd call an Assemblyman in the States. What is it you call them here?"

"MHA," said Theresa in a near-whisper, blushing as though this were a slightly daring confidence, and pronouncing the middle letter in the Newfoundland manner, as haitch.

"Yeah," said Bannister, not entirely sure what she had said. "That's it. What's his name again? Merrigan. Loyola Merrigan. You know him?"

Theresa blushed again, this time with a touch of pride. "I knows a girl in his office," she said in a slightly louder whisper.

"That so? Which office?"

Theresa looked blank and stricken, like a pupil who has been set an impossible problem in geometry by a demanding teacher.

"I mean, is she in his government office, up in the Confederation Building," Bannister prompted, "or in his law office downtown?"

"Oh. Downtown. On Water Street."

"Well, well," Bannister said. "Isn't that interesting. And does she like working for him?"

Here Theresa decided to pass on a real confidence. "She says he's some crooked," she said, and giggled.

Interesting, Bannister thought. Very interesting indeed. And possibly very useful, too. "Well, well," he said again. "What else does she say?"

Theresa was feeling less shy now. This sort of gossipy discussion of personalities was familiar ground. "Sometimes he gets right dirty with her," she said.

Even more interesting, Bannister thought. So the old reprobate likes young girls. That could come in handy. "Really?" he said, mildly. "What does she think of that?"

"Oh, she don't mind him," Theresa replied. "She's used to it now. She don't care."

Bannister decided not to press the matter any further for the moment. He would return to the conversation another time. After a few more banalities he wandered casually back into his office.

A quick check of his files confirmed what he had thought. There wasn't much there on the MHA for The Shore at all, and what there was seemed to make him out to be pretty straight. Bannister leaned back, pleased with himself. Clearly, he had just picked up something the research people, for all their box full of detail, had missed.

Half of his mind was busy turning over the possibilities that the new information opened up, but the other half kept straying to an extraneous theme— the matter-of-fact way that young Theresa had mentioned this old guy "getting dirty" with her friend. She seemed to take it for granted— treated it as a joke. The errant half of his mind wandered further into thoughts of how Theresa might react if he were to get her to work late some night, without Miss Hiscock. He began to construct another fantasy for use the next time he was chatting with Al.

He was still fully preoccupied when Schultz returned and, after exchanging a few words with the women, burst unannounced into Bannister's office. Bannister reacted with professional smoothness. He slipped the crinkly pages of the Master Plan to one side of his desk, dropped a small pile of other papers on top, and stood up, all in one casual motion. He greeted Schultz with much more cordiality than he felt, and steered him away from the desk to the coffee table in the corner.

The office door was still ajar. "Marge!" Bannister called. "Hey, Marge!" Miss Hiscock entered, her back even more ramrod-straight than usual, her lips a narrow line. The chill was almost palpable as she said, "Yes, Mr. Bannister," in her most proper tone.

Bannister didn't notice. "Bring us a couple of cups of coffee will you, Marge?" he said over his shoulder, staying between Schultz and the desk.

In moments of stress, most animals engage in what psychologists call displacement behaviour—small routine movements that have nothing to do with the cause of the strain. Uneasy cats scratch; threatened birds pick up small twigs and drop them; male public speakers, nervous about their speeches, check their flies. Miss Hiscock, aware only of an unreasoning desire to shout several words that she had never used in her life, turned to Bannister's desk and picked up a little pile of letters she had left there for him to sign, then walked stiffly out of the room.

As she reached the outer office, Bannister's voice followed her. "Marge! Cream and sugar for Schultz, okay?"

She stiffened even more. Across the room she caught Theresa watching her with a sly grin.

She strode over to the table where the girl was working, slapped down the little pile of papers and snatched an envelope from her hands.

"Really, Theresa," she snapped. "The least you could do is put the labels on straight." She peeled off the offending sticker and re-stuck it, her anger still rising. "Not that it will matter to those ignorant baymen, anyway. I expect most of them can't read!"

She might have said more, but the sudden look of cold fury in Theresa's eyes made her realize that she had already gone too far. A rural Newfoundlander may use the term "bayman" occasionally with a measure of pride, but when it is uttered by a person from the city, coupled with references to ignorance and stupidity, it can be a fighting word. And Theresa, Miss Hiscock belatedly recalled, was from The Shore. Angrier than ever, she wheeled and strode off to make the coffee.

Theresa tilted her carefully-styled head, squared her shoulders, thrust out a dimpled but firm little chin, muttered "old townie bitch!" in a voice calculated with a schoolgirl's precision to be just on the threshold of audibility, and began plotting revenge.

Her eye fell on the little pile of papers Miss Hiscock had slapped down on the table. It was about the same size as the information packages she was stuffing in the envelopes. It wasn't her fault if it was lying there, right beside the other things, was it? In seconds, the pile of papers was in an envelope, sealed, and addressed with a label, meticulously straight. That would do for a start. More would follow.

Bannister's forced affability gave Schultz a comfortable feeling that he had somehow gained the upper hand, and he chattered freely over his coffee, discussing future contracts for HIPE (Canada). Outside the closed door, Miss Hiscock and Theresa worked on in hostile silence.

At a quarter to five, Schultz's deliveryman returned and took away several boxes of envelopes for mailing. At five precisely, Theresa ostentatiously put down the envelope she had been about to seal and walked out the door without a word. A few moments later, Miss Hiscock broke with thirty years of practice and left her place of work without telling her employer she was going and asking if anything else would be required of her. At five-fifteen Schultz finally went home.

At five-fifteen and a half, Bannister returned to his desk and found the planning document gone.

When he let himself into his furnished apartment in Elizabeth Towers it was after ten. He had a violent headache and his stomach hurt, the result of drinking seven cups of coffee, smoking a full packet of cigarettes after having been off tobacco for three years, and not having had any supper.

It had been fairly easy to reconstruct what had happened, but it had taken time. Miss Hiscock had returned promptly on his telephone call, guilty and embarrassed but cooperative. Theresa had been harder to find, and was defensive and evasive. Bannister had had to mask his panic and proceed with caution. They could not, of course, be told what was at stake; on the other hand, they had to be made to realize that it was more than just the loss of a few innocuous letters.

By the time the story was pieced together, Mogul Oil's top-secret plans were making their way through the bowels of Canada Post, on their way to some anonymous householder on the Hard Shore.

VI

At the emergency meeting next morning, Bannister cut the preliminaries short— Theresa's protests that the papers were right there on the table, and how was she to know...? and Miss Hiscock's repeated assertions that never, in thirty-some years, had she ever....

"Look, never mind all that. I don't give a damn whose fault it was," he said, privately vowing to fire them both as soon as the papers were found, or— and his stomach gave a twinge at the thought— brought to public attention. "Somebody's going to get that stuff in the mail and we're going to look like assho...like idiots. Our reputation is at stake here. If this gets out we might just as well close down. None of us will have a job. Who's going to give work to an outfit that can't even send out announcements right?"

Oil people know about leaks, and they have set ways of dealing with them. Three objectives are pursued simultaneously and with equal vigour: plug the hole, contain the spill, and keep the whole thing as quiet as can be managed in the circumstances. Whether the leak is of oil or information, the procedures are the same.

Normally, batteries of experts can be called in to handle each aspect of the operation, but Bannister was in no position to do that. He had to get the planning document back before Mogul Oil or the Houston office knew it was gone, or his career would be finished.

"Okay," he said. "We've got to find out where that package went, and we've got to get it back. Fast. Now, how are we going to do it?"

There were no quick answers. Several hundred packages were still to be sent, and the names on their stickers could be eliminated from consideration, but that still left something over three thousand people who might be about to receive a rather unusual piece of mail. And Schultz's random computer programme ensured that the recipient could be in any of the score of small communities on The Hard Shore.

Suggestions of advertisements in the paper and announcements on the radio were quickly discarded. Bannister wanted no public attention. Theresa, getting into what she felt was the spirit of the thing, suggested turning it into a kind of lottery: whoever got the lucky package would receive a five hundred dollar prize. But how can you operate a lottery without telling people it is going on? Bannister's state of mind was not improved by having their discussion interrupted by another cheery visit from Schultz, and by the fact that they had to complete the mailing of the remaining kits to maintain the appearance that all was well. Finally, late in the afternoon, he decided on a strategy. It wasn't much, but it was the best he could come up with.

"Okay," he said. "Today's Friday. The kits were mailed yesterday. Monday morning the three of us are going to be out there on this godda...on this Hard Shore place, and we're going to do a door-to-door canvass.

"We'll tell people we're doing a survey to find out how many people got the kits and read the material. We'll ask to see the kits and we'll ask a few questions. Make it sound official, like some stupid godda...like something Schultz might dream up.

"And maybe we can work in that idea of Theresa's too. Yeah. We'll tell them that some of the packages are special, see, and anybody who's got one of those could be entitled to a cash prize.

"That'll get a bit of word-of-mouth going, and maybe speed things up a bit. Tell 'em to tell their friends, and leave 'em our phone number. I'll get an answering service to handle the calls— no, maybe we better just get a message tape.

"And maybe— just maybe— we'll get lucky. You won't have any trouble recognizing the stuff if you see it. And if you see it, grab it. Promise them anything, but just get that stuff in here. Don't fool around reading it, just bring it in. Okay?"

In his effort to convince the women that the job was not impossible, he managed to convince himself that they had a chance. After all, he told himself, nobody pays much attention to stuff like that when it comes in the mail. And these are just ordinary people, mostly— the planning document wouldn't mean much to them unless they sat down and really read it. Of course, some of them might just throw the whole thing away. Nothing we can do about that, except get out there and get started as quick as we can. If anybody stuffed it in a wood-stove, of course, the flash-paper would go off— they'd remember that and probably mention it....

Only the three of them knew that anything had gone wrong, and only he knew how badly wrong it was. He had impressed on Miss Hiscock and Theresa the need for secrecy. The Shore was rural, and an hour and a half from St. John's, so their word-of-mouth campaign would not attract any attention in the city, at least for a while. By then they might have turned up the missing document. It wasn't a great chance, but it was the only one available.

In fact, though, the mishap was already less secret than he thought it was.

Theresa had released part of it when she was the only one who knew about it. She was in the habit of meeting some of her telephone friends in a downtown bar occasionally after work. None of them liked to drink very much, but since most of them were still too young to do it legally, meeting in a bar made them feel very grown-up and sophisticated. Besides, they were usually joined by young men in similar circumstances— "management trainees" at Woolco, and junior clerks from government offices. Within an hour after revenging herself on Miss Hiscock, she was telling the story at the top of her voice in competition with ear-splitting rock music amid the mock-western corral posts and plastic Mexican saddles of the Brand X Saloon, and she was called upon to repeat it several times as newcomers joined the group.

Miss Hiscock had passed it on later the same evening in strictest confidence, to assuage her feelings of guilt and embarrassment. On several nights a week, she talked on the telephone with the only person left in the world— apart from Bannister, who didn't count— to call her by her first name. Her full first name.

She and Stella Mercer had begun these regular conversations when they were classmates at Bishop Spencer Academy, when Stella was not Mercer, but Pike. They had not done it for several years when Miss Hiscock went away to school in England, and then Stella had met and married George Mercer, a plump and rather stodgy retail merchant whom Miss Hiscock did not like, but as the Mercer children grew toward alienated adolescence and George began to spend more evenings at his shop and meetings of his various service clubs, the old pattern was re-established, and continued.

Miss Hiscock felt a little better after telling Stella, who had already heard a great deal about Bannister's boorishness and Theresa's sullen intransigence. And although Stella knew it was a confidence, she could see no harm in mentioning it to George over breakfast. It was rare enough that she had anything new to say to him.

In spite of Bannister's urgent demands that the whole thing had to be kept quiet, neither Miss Hiscock nor Theresa felt any sense of wrongdoing. Ideas of secrecy are relative, after all. Neither of them would have told Schultz, or anybody else they knew to be directly involved.

On the other hand, neither of them really believed that anything could ever be completely secret. Their whole life experience had taught them that such a thing was impossible.

St. John's is an old city, capital of an old society. Generations of kinship ties and school friendships connect its parts and link it with the surrounding countryside in ways quite different from the typical big North American city where everybody comes from somewhere else. Information travels along these links with astonishing speed. Rumours that are bandied about over cocktails in fashionable living rooms in Bally Haly often bear a striking resemblance to those that are traded over beer glasses in Water Street bars. And although each teller tends to add a few embellishments for dramatic effect, the rumours often contain a substantial measure of truth.

Even as Bannister and his little staff prepared for their assault on The Shore, a version of their dilemma was enlivening the morning coffee-break from Bowrings to the Confederation building cafeteria.

"Funny thing about that oil outfit and those papers, eh? Oh, didn't you hear? Well, the way I heard it...."

The details were necessarily vague. There was some disagreement over which oil outfit was involved and what the missing papers contained, but those were gaps that could easily be filled. In Bowrings the consensus was that they were a confidential statement of Mogul's corporate profits. In the Confederation Building they were known to be confirmation of a big new strike on the Hibernia Field.

VII

Father Morrissey was opening his mail.

It was a time of the day he always enjoyed: a quiet half hour in mid-morning with the study door securely closed and his housekeeper, Mrs. Fagan, instructed not to disturb him for anything but the direst of emergencies.

Items that might upset his cosy peace— overdue bills, estimates of repairs to the church roof, and the like— he stacked at one side of his desk for later attention. If there were treats, like a letter from a friend or a magazine article he wanted to read, he would savour them at leisure. If there were none, he would simply sit and enjoy a pot of tea and a quiet smoke in front of the window that looked down, weather permitting, over the houses and sheds to the fish plant and the little harbour that made up the village of St. Cyril's, seat of the parish of St. Jude and centre of the area known as the Hard Shore.

This morning there were no personal letters and no journals, but his eye was caught by a large brown envelope emblazoned with the logo of Mogul Oil. At first he put it with the bills, but curiosity prevailed. He slit it open and scanned the contents, and the atmosphere of peace was irrevocably shattered. He pushed back his chair, closed his eyes, and took several deep breaths in an effort to prevent himself from falling into the deadly sin of Anger.

Even with the addition of a silent prayer, his effort was without success. He slammed the contents of the envelope down on the desk with a force that scattered bills in all directions and shot a storm of cigarette ashes out over the carpet. After a few more deep breaths he began, as a minor penance, gloomily to contemplate the rest of his catalogue of sins.

Not Lust— or not seriously. He had come to terms with that, so his older colleagues assured him, as well as could be expected. Neither his housekeeper nor the ladies of the parish, nor even his well-meaning maiden aunts in St. John's, were good enough cooks to tempt him to Gluttony. No, the besetting sins of Gerard Morrissey, he reflected sadly, continued to be Envy, Pride of a rather particular kind, and the one that had set off this familiar review.

It was particularly annoying that these sins arose out of a sincere desire to do good. Gerard Morrissey was no grubber after power or privilege: it was not the bishop he envied, and certainly not his bourgeois brother Frank in Grand Falls, with his fancy house and plump wife and holidays in Florida. Father Morrissey's ambition was of quite another kind, and the people he envied were of an altogether different stamp.

He had never doubted his vocation. All he had ever wanted to be was a priest. But he wanted, with equal or even greater fervour, to be what he could not help but think of as a *relevant* priest, and that thought in itself could be construed as sinful.

Even before he had gone to university at St. Francis Xavier he had been inspired by stories of the founders of the Antigonish Movement, Fathers Coady and Tompkins, organizing fishermen and farmers to fight the big corporations that held them in poverty. At the university he studied co-ops and credit unions until he was sure he could organize one in his sleep— and, in fact, had frequently done just that in vivid dreams in which he re-enacted the achievements of his heroes. At the seminary, he was enthralled by the priests from Latin American missions who occasionally lectured: intense, committed clerics who talked more about social justice than theology.

But with his ordination, no call came for Gerry Morrissey to organize the peasants of Peru or minister to beleaguered guerrillas in Guatemala. He found himself instead in a Toronto suburb, curate to an elderly eccentric who was obsessed with the idea that all the liberalizing movements within the Church had but one goal—to institute a policy that would not merely permit, but would require priests to marry.

When he was finally posted back to Newfoundland, the chronic shortage of clergy caused him to be moved frequently, relieving in a series of rural parishes, never in one place long enough to more than dabble in the kind of work he wanted to do. Finally, a reasonably permanent appointment on the Hard Shore seemed to open the way at last.

As in any Newfoundland parish, unemployment was high and incomes low. The dimensions of peoples' lives were controlled by government policies set in St. John's and Ottawa, and by the vagaries of the fish market in Boston. The potential seemed great, but after nearly ten years Father Morrissey was no nearer achieving his ideals than he had been in suburban Toronto.

The trouble was that the many undoubted problems of the parish were mostly merely local manifestations, flaws in much larger systems, beyond the reach of those most affected. Besides, the lives of the people had always, since the days of early settlement, been controlled by forces beyond their grasp, from the weather to the machinations of remote bureaucracies. They resisted when they could, but mostly they had learned to endure, to make the best of whatever came along.

This attitude, in Father Morrissey's view, made the whole society dangerously vulnerable. At the root of all the problems was a simple shortage of productive economic activity: that much was obvious to anybody. The solution, equally clear, lay in what could broadly be termed economic development. And that was where things began to get difficult.

He still had his dreams. Often he would imagine himself back at the seminary as a distinguished visitor, lecturing on community development to a serious, fascinated class of neophytes.

"We see economic development as the cure," he would say, as the student priests scribbled industriously in their notebooks, "but what of the side-effects? Are there not some cures that are worse than the disease? Is it not true that some kinds of development in a community can destroy the very things that make it a community in the first place?

"It is not just development that it needed," he would go on after a dramatic pause, "but *appropriate* development!"

Usually, at this point, his fantasy would skip to the end of the speech, in which he gave a picture of the Hard Shore transformed into a happy, industrious and prosperous rural Eden. The students and their teachers would not actually applaud, but their expressions would show that they were restraining themselves only out of consideration for the well-known modesty and humility of the lecturer.

These fantasies left him feeling embarrassed and guilty, like one who has been practising a secret vice. The missing part of the lecture would prey on his mind.

In his weakest moments he was haunted by the thought that the whole thing was insoluble. By contrast, the problems of the Third World seemed enviably— chalk up another sin— clear cut. The stakes and the odds were incalculably greater, but they made the path of virtue easy to see. He subscribed to the *New Internationalist*, took a great interest in Latin America and Africa, and read a lot about Liberation Theology.

Father Morrissey rolled himself another cigarette. He had begun the practice out of a desire to identify with the workers: it had escaped his notice that most of them smoked ready-made, and by now it was completely ingrained as a habit. He bought his tobacco and papers a packet at a time in strict rotation among several small stores in the parish: he did not wish to show any favouritism, and calling in at one of the shops almost every day was a way of keeping in touch with his people.

Since he smoked an obscure Dutch blend used by almost nobody else, the stores had to order it specially; and since they could only get it by the case, the tobacco was always dry and crumbly by the time he bought it. As a consequence, his cigarettes gave off little showers of glowing embers, and clothing he had worn for any length of time was dotted down the front with small black-edged holes. Outdoors in a breeze, he often streamed sparks in a manner that had led one of his parishioners to compare him to a "shaggin' Roman candle," and a Protestant clergyman of his acquaintance to joke about his being an ever-present reminder of the fires of Hell.

As so often happens to even the most virtuous of people, reflection on his sins shaded almost imperceptibly into an occasion for practising them. He patted absently at a glowing shred of tobacco on his old cardigan and thought bitterly about the opportunities that seemed to come so easily to others: that fellow from Cape Breton, for instance, and the other one from Saskatchewan, sitting in the House of Commons for the NDP....

Of course, the Holy Father had put a stop to that sort of thing, at least in Canada, at least for the time being. But think of the Nicaraguan clergy in the revolutionary government!

That, admittedly, is a totally different situation. But think of the nuns on the Social Action Committee in St. John's, organizing public meetings in support of strikers, walking on picket lines! And that big fellow from the West Coast, working full-time with the fishermen's union! Father Morrissey would much rather wear that man's baseball cap with the union crest than a cardinal's biretta, and rather be known by his affectionate nickname of The Codfather than have any title the hierarchy had to offer.

He sighed, and with an effort pulled his mind back from this unprofitable but familiar course. Envy again.

He glared balefully at the papers from Mogul Oil. There was, after all, such a thing as righteous anger. It was damned insulting. No other word for it. Here they are announcing a big public meeting; local dignitaries and functionaries all to be present and say a few words, information to be given, regional development to be discussed, and nowhere a mention of the Reverend G. Morrissey.

Not an oversight. No, a deliberate omission, no question about that. No question about who was responsible, either. There it was in black and white on the first page: "Meeting arranged with the cooperation of the Hard Shore Association for Regional Economic Development."

Yes. Pete Kelly and the rest of that development-at-any-price crowd knew well enough how their parish priest felt about big multinational corporations. They'd be whining around for a few crumbs of jobs while the oil barons turned the whole of Newfoundland into a wasteland of...here his imagination failed. He was not quite certain what the wasteland would look like, but he was sure it would be unpleasant.

Well, so much for the quiet half hour. He stuffed his tobacco and papers into his shirt pocket and went out for a breath of air.

Down on the government wharf, next to the fish plant, a little group of men were enjoying the spring sunshine. "There's Father," said one, squinting up the hill. "Out for a stroll. I wonder should we call out the Fire Department?"

"I believes he's gettin' worse," said another. "The other day I got to the lee of him outside the church and he near set me alight. He was givin' off sparks like a welding torch."

"Don't you be talkin'," said a third. "The other week when me old mother was took bad, God love her, the missus wouldn't let me call him in to give her the Last Rites. 'If we calls him in to her,' she says, 'I'll have to give him a cup of tea. And if I gives him a cup of tea,' she says, 'he'll have a smoke. And if he has a smoke,' she says, 'he'll ruin me new shag carpet. Hold off a bit and maybe she'll rally.' She did, too, poor old soul, so the carpet's safe for the time bein'."

"Keep an eye on him," said Pete Kelly. "If he comes down this way, I'm going to dodge off. I don't want to see him just now."

"Don't worry, Pete, boy," said. the first speaker. "There's enough of us here to put you out if he catches fire to you. We could just throw you over the wharf."

"Very funny," said Kelly. "I'm more worried about what he's going to have to say to me."

"What've you been up to now, Pete? Must have been somethin' pretty bad, for you to be feared to face him. He's a decent stick, Father is, as long as you stays clear of the sparks. You must have some bad conscience."

"You just mind your own conscience," Kelly said, "and I'll look after mine. No, the thing is, there's some announcements of a meeting in the mail. We'll all be getting them in the next day or so...."

"That offshore oil thing?" one of the group said. "I got one of them this mornin'. What's all that about, Pete?"

"Well, it's just a public meeting. The Association is helping to organize it. Fellas from Mogul Oil is going to come down and talk about oil development."

One of the other men grunted disgustedly. "If I never hears no more about that it won't bother me none. They've been goin' on about oil development this fifteen year, and there's nothin' after happenin' yet that's worth a pinch. The only people that makes anything out of it is them that holds the meetings."

"But what's it got to do with Father?" someone broke in. "Well," said Kelly, a little uncomfortably, "the fact is, he hasn't been invited to take part. There'll be a few people on the stage, see—the Member, and the President of the Development Association, and me, as Coordinator—but he isn't one of them. And he's not going to be pleased. He's going to get the announcement one of these mornings, and I don't want to be around to hear about it when he does."

"That don't seem fair," said one of the men. "Sure, he's the parish priest, ain't he? And he's always goin' on about development. He'd drive you to the drink with it. You'd think he'd be top of the list."

"That," said Kelly, "is the whole trouble, right there. Now, don't get me wrong. He's a decent little man altogether. As good a parish priest as any I've seen, and better than most, considering what some of them get up to. The only trouble is, on the subject of community development, he's cracked."

"Like his grandfather," said a wavery, thin old voice with a wheezy chuckle.

The men looked at one another apprehensively. The speaker was Brendan O'Leary, the second-oldest resident on the Shore, whose toothless, extravagantly wrinkled face had appeared several times along with dilapidated fish flakes on brochures designed to attract Mainland tourists to "the real Newfoundland."

Usually, he sat among the little group of idling men in distant silence, as though posing for yet another photograph. Their apprehension was caused by the fact that when O'Leary did speak he usually went on at interminable length. They feared what was coming, but politeness demanded that they respond. "His grandfather?" said one, after a pause.

"Mad Jack Morrissey," the old man said. "There was a man who was cracked for sure and certain."

They had all heard the story many times before. "He belonged to Placentia Bay some place, didn't he?" someone prompted, trying to hurry things along.

"Black Island," old Brendan confirmed. "Black Island, Placentia Bay."

"And he run a schooner aground...," said someone else, as though on cue.

"My son, he run schooners aground from here to the Labrador," said O'Leary with satisfaction. "He was famous for it. His trouble, you see, was he saw things."

"Visions, like?"

"Visions." The old man turned his eyes up piously. "Now, I'm not a man to scoff at visions, but Jack Morrissey went to hell with it altogether. He run the *Eleanor Jane* ashore in broad daylight in Witless Bay. Said he saw the Holy Family standin' on Jimmy White's stage, and was haulin' in for a closer look.

"And then,"– the old man's voice was heavy with drama– "and then there was the *Eileen*." He hawked, spat, closed his eyes, threw back his head and began to sing in a startlingly tuneless croak:

Ye ladies and gentlemen, hear me sad tale;
It will make ye to tremble and turn your cheeks pale,
When ye hears of the terrible sights that I seen,
When I shipped with Mad Morrissey on the *Eileen*!

The men shifted nervously and several looked at their watches. The ballad of Mad Jack Morrissey, intact, could last a good twenty minutes. They breathed easier when, instead of going on, O'Leary opened his eyes and gave another wheezy chuckle.

"One of them young fellas that was down here last year from the University with his recordin' machine thought it was Matt Morrison, but he knows nothin' about it. Mad Jack Morrissey, it was. I knows."

"Father don't see visions, though," said someone, taking advantage of a pause to divert the conversation back to its theme. "He don't even believe in most of 'em. Do you know, he told me...."

"I'd be happier if he did," said Pete Kelly. "The kind of thing he gets on with is a damn sight worse. I'll tell you boys something, now, that I never told nobody before, and maybe you'll understand what I mean."

There was an anticipatory shuffling, and attention turned from the ancient O'Leary, who resumed his usual detached, distant stare with an air of satisfaction.

"You remember— oh, ten years ago, say— just after Father come here, when we nearly got that factory?"

"I think so," said one. "They was going to turn out them little plastic knives and forks they gives you at the take-outs with your plate of chips, wasn't they?"

"Bloody useless little things," someone else put in.

"That's it," said Kelly. "And useless they may be, but when you think of all the take-outs in Newfoundland, and the way people are heaving chips and gravy into themselves every day of the week, and a little plastic fork and knife with every order, you've got to admit a factory like that would be a proper gold mine!"

There was a murmur of general assent to this proposition.

"Well, I'll tell you," Kelly went on. "They come down here from the Mainland. Two fellas in fancy suits with a rented car from St. John's. Big gold rings on their fingers.

"I showed 'em around, and they loved it. See, a factory like that makes a nice bit of waste chemicals and that kind of thing, and when they saw the Brook they was delighted. 'Just run a pipe in there,' they says, 'and she's all washed out to sea.'

"DREE was on the go then, and they could've got a grant for the building, and the Province would've gave them a subsidy on the Hydro, and when I told them about the unemployment rate, and the minimum wage— well, you could hardly hold 'em back. I tell you, boys, I thought we had that factory sewed up in a brin bag. And that's when I made my big mistake.

"See, Father was new here at that time, eh? I didn't know what he was like. So, I'm trying to impress these fellas. 'Oh, yes,' I says, 'They're good, religious people here,' I says. 'They won't give you no trouble.' And, like you would, I takes them up to meet the priest."

73

Kelly's audience was rapt. A new story is a thing to be savoured. There were nods of approval and encouragement.

"Well," Kelly said, "that was the end of that. No sooner did he shake hands with them than he started firin' questions at them: Didn't their company have a factory in South America or some jeezly place where the workers was dyin' like flies from the plastic fumes, and bein' paid ten cents an hour for the privilege? And wasn't it their company was run out of Ontario for killin' off horses and cows with the pollution? And how did they feel about a union?

"My sons, they couldn't get back into their car fast enough, and I never seen them again!

"And then, to cap it off, he come to me afterwards. 'I'm some glad you brought them fellas around to see me, Pete, boy,' he says. 'You let me know if they ever comes back and we'll organize a march on the Confederation Building!' Sure, he was all for havin' people lay down in the road in front of the bulldozers if they tried to start building her."

There were further murmurs and head-shakings.

"I heard they got set up later in New Brunswick," Kelly concluded. "They went broke or something later, but that's beside the point. Think of the jobs we could've had setting her up!"

They all looked up toward the church and Father Morrissey's house.

"You never know," someone said.

"You don't, for sure," said another, and several spat reflectively.

"So that's why he isn't going to have anything to do with this oil meeting," said Kelly. "Not if I have anything to do with it. Is that him comin' down the hill? I'm off now, boys. Take 'er easy."

VIII

Although they had agreed on a common approach, each member of the staff of HIPE (Canada) set about the search for the missing papers somewhat differently. Bannister and Miss Hiscock were both anxious and apprehensive, though in different ways and for different reasons. Theresa, once the uncomfortable business of admitting what had happened was behind her, threw herself into the task with youthful enthusiasm generated by the novelty of it all. Even while her seniors were laboriously working out the details, she was laying her own plans.

The first step, as soon as she got off work, was a call to Carmelita Slaney, one of her closest friends, who was still living at home on The Shore. Carmelita expressed mock surprise.

"Treece! Jeez, girl, you're a stranger these days. I thought you'd forgot all about us now you're in St. John's!"

"Oh, I been a bit busy, Carm. You knows how it is. I got this job with an oil outfit, see...."

"Right, I seen your mother the other week, and she was tellin' me. Still livin' at your aunt Joan's?"

"Yeah," said Theresa. "For now. I'm gettin' me own place soon. Then you can come and visit. You workin'?"

"Not right now, girl. I got my stamps in at the fish plant, so I'm on the pogey. Listen, why don't you come home for the weekend? We could...."

After these preliminaries, it was simple for Theresa to present an edited version of the events that had led up to the call and a proposal for joint action. Carmelita, as usual, was game for any diversion.

"Sure, girl. It'll be a grand bit of fun. Jackie's old Chev is still runnin', more or less. Of course, if we gets Jackie and the Chev, we gets Phonse too, you knows that."

"I know," said Theresa, without enthusiasm. "Can't be helped, I suppose."

"Okay," said Carmelita. "You say your boss is droppin' you off in St. Cyril's at ten on Monday. That's awful early to get Jackie out of bed, but I'll do me best. We'll meet you down by the take-out. See ya."

On Monday morning Theresa had to wait for only a half an hour before the rusty old Chev arrived bearing Carmelita, her lanky, leather-jacketed boyfriend Jackie O'Byrne and Jackie's cousin and inseparable companion, Phonse. Quickly, the young people worked out their own variant on the house to house canvass planned in the HIPE (Canada) offices.

"The way I sees it," Jackie said judiciously, "We don't want to make too big a thing of this cash prize business. Maybe we shouldn't mention it at all. Why, suppose somebody hears about that, and they've got the papers, and they calls up your boss, Treece. My Jeez, there'd be the money gone and us not even gettin' a look at it! Let's just see if we can find them papers. Maybe then we can...sort of share it, like. How much is it, anyway, Treece?"

Theresa was vague on the point. In fact, Bannister had not actually mentioned a figure, but in any case she would not have wanted to be overly specific. Knowing Jackie's inclinations and chronic want of money, she thought it best not to put too much temptation in his way. Some, but not too much. For the same reason, she did not mention the money

Bannister had allowed her for the day's expenses. She'd see how things went first, then maybe give them a bit of a surprise.

Almost everybody on the Shore was related to at least one of them, so they agreed to share the duties of spokesperson. The first call of the day set the pattern for the others.

"Mornin' Aunt Bride," said Jackie. "Grand day."

Aunt Bride was hanging out some laundry, and spoke around a clothespin. "Hmph. Mornin', Jackie. It ain't rainin' yet, if that's what you mean. But I'm surprised you're up to know about it. Your bed catch fire, or what?"

"Ha, ha. Oh, I gets up now and again. When I has to. Listen, did you get a letter in the mail at all, from Mogul Oil?"

His aunt took the clothespin out of her mouth and looked at him narrowly. "And what's that got to do with you?"

"Well, I'm just givin' the girls here a hand. You knows Carm, of course...," Aunt Bride's expression suggested that she knew more about Carmelita than she wanted to "...and I guess you knows Treece Foley...."

"Theresa Foley, is that you? Mary Foley's girl, from St. Kevin's?"

Theresa's demeanour was as modest and demure as ever Miss Hiscock could have wished. "Yes, Mrs. O'Byrne."

"You're the oldest, right?"

"No, Mrs. O'Byrne. Alice and Eileen are both older than me."

"My God, how time does go by! It's just the other day you was havin' your first communion. Or maybe it was one of your sisters. How's your mother? I don't expect she'd approve of you hangin' around with our Jackie, here."

"Aw, come on, Aunt Bride," said Jackie, "I ain't that bad. Give us a kiss." His aunt fended him off with a handful of wet clothes. "I'm just helpin' her out. See, poor old Treece works for the outfit that sent them letters out. Everybody on The Shore got sent one, and she was stuffin' them in the envelopes. Thousands of 'em. And it seems she got mixed up, and put some other papers in one of 'em by mistake."

The four young people held their breaths and crossed their fingers. They had decided right from the beginning that the story concocted by Bannister and Miss Hiscock was too cumbersome. This was one of those rare situations where something very close to the truth was probably the best approach, but it had its risks. They knew that they had reached the most delicate point of the interview.

Aunt Bride was as quick on the uptake as they expected. "Hmph," she said. "Must be some important if they sends you out lookin' for them. What are they?"

Carmelita now chimed in, as demure as Theresa. "It ain't that they're so important, Mrs. O'Byrne. It's just that if Treece can't get them back she's going to lose her job for sure."

Here, too, the young people had decided to stick close to truth. Hadn't Bannister said that if the papers stayed lost nobody at HIPE (Canada) would have a job? If people misunderstood, and got the impression that Theresa was trying on her own to cover a mistake, wouldn't that only make them more willing to help?

As they had expected, it was an appeal that no mother with growing children in chronically job-short Newfoundland could resist. "Oh, well," Aunt Bride said, with another suspicious look at her nephew, "I believes we did get some kind of thing. Your uncle might've hove it out, but I'll go look."

In this manner they moved quickly through the hamlet. In many cases they could by-pass the householder altogether by sending a convenient youngster home to whip the information kit off the kitchen table and produce it for inspection. By supper time they had not found the missing papers, but had racked up an impressive total of completed investigations— many more than Bannister and Miss Hiscock had planned for.

Theresa, well pleased, used her expense money to buy hamburgers all around, put a few dollars worth of gas in the Chev, and supply the boys with a half a dozen beer. Altogether, it had been a highly successful day.

To say that Miss Hiscock had not been looking forward to the day's activities would be true only in the figurative sense. She had, in fact, been anticipating them with so much anxiety that she had hardly slept at all.

Miss Hiscock was very much a woman of the city. She was familiar enough with outport communities: drove through them on outings, found them picturesque, even on occasion professed admiration for the hardy way of life of their occupants. But to actually go from door to door in one of them, knocking, asking questions...the whole idea filled her with dread. Only a sense of guilt over her share in the loss of the papers drove her to it. She put on stout, low-heeled shoes, a tailored tweed suit and light raincoat with matching hat, and arrived in Walsh's Cove precisely at ten o'clock.

She had driven through the community countless times, but never before stopped. Now she contemplated it with rising panic. Like hundreds of its kind, it had come into being long before roads were built, or even thought of. In the thirty years since the highway had been put through, the village had been slowly re-arranging itself along the ribbon, but its sixty-odd houses were still widely scattered over knobbly terrain, perched on rock outcrops, tucked into a hillside cleft, or centred on tiny, sheep-nibbled plots of sparse grass, facing in whatever direction they chose and connected by a network of lanes and tracks.

Old, four-square, flat-roofed, two-story houses stood sturdily overlooking new, suburban style bungalows with wide vinyl siding and elaborately decorated aluminum storm doors opening into mid-air where front steps were meant to be; a few mansard roofs with curved dormers peeped from behind sheltering trees, and everywhere there were sheds, equipment the uses of which Miss Hiscock could not imagine, nets hung on fences, and boats on cradles surprisingly far from the water's edge.

Almost all the houses were in good repair and neatly painted, some in startling but nonetheless cheerful colours.

Picturesque, to be sure. But she had no idea where to begin. The point had not occurred to her until now, but there were no house numbers, and no street signs. A remarkable number of the names on her list were Walsh.

Only one house that she could see from behind the wheel of her car advertised any sort of identity. It was also the only one visible that was in a state of decay: a sagging, unpainted, tumbledown cottage almost engulfed by a wild growth of elderly trees. On one drunken gate-post was a faded, hand-lettered sign saying "W. Walsh." Beneath, in smaller letters, was something that might once have said "saws filed." There were two William Walshes on her list, and one Walter.

Calling on all her not inconsiderable reserves of determination, Miss Hiscock pushed past the rickety gate, desperately praying that there would not be a dog. A snarling, barking sort of dog would be terrible; a smelly, slobbering, effusively friendly one nearly as bad.

The peeling front door stood ajar. She knocked firmly, but not as loudly as she had intended. Nothing happened.

She knocked again, louder, and a muffled voice said, "Come in. 'Tis open."

Miss Hiscock stepped gingerly into a shadowy, low-ceilinged room full of vague shapes and curious, dismaying smells. As her eyes adjusted, she perceived in a corner a small, very old man peering at her over a fringe of grey beard stubble that almost exactly matched the tufts of stuffing that protruded here and there from the upholstered chair that surrounded him. He was wearing grimy work clothes and an incongruous bright yellow baseball cap with "Labatt's Blue" on the front. As if in deliberate contradiction, he held an open bottle of Dominion Ale in his lap.

"I'm looking for Mr. William Walsh," she said.

The old man contemplated her for some moments in silence. "Old Bill," he said finally, "is on the beer."

"I see," said Miss Hiscock, conscious of the inadequacy of her response. "Do you expect him...ah...back?"

"On the beer," the old man said, and belched reflectively. Then, gathering himself with an effort, he leaned forward. "If you've come about the land, 'twill do you no good. 'Tis mine by right." He belched again and squinted up at Miss Hiscock. "You knows me sister?" he asked, challengingly.

"Well, no," Miss Hiscock said. "No. Actually...."

"She'd tell you." He nodded. "Only she's dead now, God rest her."

"I'm sorry," said Miss Hiscock. "Well, perhaps I'll come back another...."

"Dead these fifteen year," he said with finality, "and Old Bill is on the beer." He closed his eyes and seemed to go to sleep.

Outside in the road, Miss Hiscock suppressed an urgent desire to look around to see if anyone were watching, and decided to go into the small store across the street, only momentarily deterred by noticing that the proprietor's name was also advertised as Walsh.

"I was in the little house over there," she told the man behind the counter. "I was looking for Mr. William Walsh."

There was no immediate answer. "There was an old man there...."

"That'd be him," the storekeeper replied, nodding.

"He seemed to be drunk," Miss Hiscock said, trying unsuccessfully not to sound prim.

"Then that'd be him for sure."

"I couldn't seem to get much sense out of him."

"No," the storekeeper agreed. "Nor would you if he was sober." He was observing her carefully. "You're from the Welfare, I expect?" While Miss Hiscock was trying to decide whether this assumption was offensive or complimentary he went on: "It's a mortal sin, how some people around here does with the Welfare. Not many, but some."

He was about to expand on this theme when Miss Hiscock interrupted. "I'm not with the Welfare. I'm... ah...conducting a survey. For Mogul Oil. I have a list here...." She held it out for his inspection. Somehow she could not remember the phrases she had worked out during her sleepless night. The storekeeper gave the list a cursory glance and nodded, waiting for further information. She thought he looked rather pained.

She was right. He was suffering from a reaction that many middle-aged men— and some younger ones — often experienced in her presence, though she was completely unaware of it.

Miss Hiscock had spent her life trying to do things properly. She dressed carefully, appropriately, and well. She kept her steel-grey hair precisely and attractively styled. She ate, drank, slept, and exercised in what she would term a "sensible" manner, so her complexion and figure both belied her age. In her youth she had been too angular, too sharp-edged, to be attractive, but time had softened the angles and turned the edges into smoother contours. The rigidly erect posture that had once been stiff and forbidding now gave her movements grace and even elegance.

The pained expression on the storekeeper's face came from an effort, wholly unconscious on his part, to hold his own shoulders back, push out his chest, and pull in his protuberant belly.

"You see," she said, "I need to get in touch with all the householders. Perhaps you could tell me...."

82

The storekeeper was looking over her shoulder, out the window of the shop. "If you wants to know anything about the people in this town, this man comin' now is the man you should see. He owns the fish plant. Knows more about the people around here than they does themselves."

Miss Hiscock turned as the man in question entered the shop. His appearance, at least, was reassuring: he was about her own age; tall, trim, neatly turned out in a sports jacket, slacks with a knife-edged crease, crisp shirt, and discreetly patterned tie. He was also wearing a hat. She liked to see a man wearing a hat. Too many, these days, didn't bother— and too many of those who did wore those ridiculous little shrunken things with ludicrous bunches of feathers at the side, like Swiss alpinists. This one, in some way difficult to pinpoint, was just right.

Not only that, but as the man entered he lifted his hand, raised the hat, looked directly at her and said "Good morning." There was nothing flamboyant about it: it was an easy, practised gesture of old-fashioned courtesy that fit perfectly with his appearance. She responded appropriately, and he turned to the counter.

"'Morning Walt. Looks as though it will turn fine later on." His voice was firm and direct, but softened by the lilt of The Shore. All around, Miss Hiscock thought, he seemed very...competent. It was an adjective of highest praise in her vocabulary.

"It does so, Mr. Callahan," Walt agreed. "I was just tellin' this lady," he went on, "that she should have a word with you. She's somethin' to do with the oil...."

The newcomer turned to Miss Hiscock again, and this time removed his hat altogether. "I'm Patrick Callahan," he said, and extended his hand. Miss Hiscock took it and introduced herself, wondering briefly she should add "Miss" in front of Marjorie.

She was surprised to realize that somewhere in the few moments since Mr. Callahan had appeared she had made up her mind that she could not tell this man the story that had been concocted in the HIPE (Canada) offices, and could not represent herself as trudging door-to-door around this charming little village asking to see people's mail.

"It's rather complicated to explain," she began, and hesitated.

"Well," Callahan said, "perhaps you'd like to walk across to my office. It's in the fish plant, just down there. Perhaps I could offer you a cup of tea, and you could tell me. I'll just be a moment."

As they left the shop, she noticed that it did indeed look as though the day would turn fine.

Later, on the telephone to Stella, she gave an account of how things had turned out. "Really, Stella, I didn't know what I was going to do. There was that horrible little drunk man, and the storekeeper was no help. I just couldn't face the thought of going around banging on people's doors. So when this man from the fish plant arrived...."

"What's he like?" Stella asked.

"Oh, he was a tremendous help. I told him the whole story, pretty well...," she had a mild pang of guilt, recalling how she had emphasized Theresa's role in losing the papers, and had left the suggestion that her own motive was mainly to help the girl "...and he was very understanding. You see, he employs almost everybody in the place— everybody who has a job, that is. He got one of his employees to ask everybody who was at work, and some of them went home at lunch time and brought the envelopes back with them, and he's going to...."

Stella interrupted with something remarkably like a giggle. "Yes, but what's he *like*? What's his name?"

Miss Hiscock hesitated for a fraction of a second. "Callahan," she said, her voice as expressionless as she could make it.

Stella gave what would in an adolescent be termed a squeal. "Oh, Marjorie! I'll bet he went to St. Bon's. Or maybe even St. Pat's. You know what we used to say about *them*."

Miss Hiscock did know. Among the girls at Bishop Spencer, Catholic boys were reputed to be interested in "only one thing." At the time, Miss Hiscock had not been entirely certain about the details of what that one thing entailed, and was incredulous and shocked at the explanations offered by more worldly classmates, but the reputation and the somewhat exotic mysteries of their religion made the boys from St. Bonaventure's the object of endless fascinated speculation.

"Really, Stella!" she said. "What a thing to say! If you are going to...."

"What's his first name?" Stella asked, undeterred.

Another moment of hesitation. "Patrick."

"And I suppose they call him Paddy," said Stella. "Is he married?"

"Patrick," Miss Hiscock repeated, in a controlled voice. "And as a matter of fact— although I can't imagine why you would be interested in such a thing— he's a widower. His wife died two years ago."

The conversation went on in this vein for some time.

Bannister also began his search in a local store. After dropping Theresa off he drove the length of The Shore. It was the first time he had actually seen his Target Area, and while his professional memory was clicking observations into place with the mass of data he had absorbed from his files, he grew more and more dismayed at the prospect of conducting a house-to-house search, with two untrained assistants, and in comparative secrecy. The maps and photographs, accurate as they were, had not quite prepared him for the reality of the way houses and communities were spread around the terrain.

It was after eleven when he drew up in Parsons Arm, situated on a steep-sided cove on a little peninsula jutting out from The Shore. He parked in front of a low frame building marked J.A. BISHOP & SONS, GENERAL MERCHANTS. As he got out, looked around and began to mount the steps, he was watched from inside with interest by a stocky, square man with a shiny bald head.

The shop was small and jammed to the rafters with every conceivable kind of merchandise. The proprietor greeted Bannister affably and offered some predictable remarks on the weather. "Having a look around, are you? It's a grand little place, Parsons Arm!"

"Yes," Bannister replied. "Yes, it is. Very nice. I'm...."

"American!" the storekeeper said delightedly, as though he could not think of anything more exciting. "Could tell as soon as you spoke. I worked for the Americans when I was a youngster. During the War. At Fort Pepperell, in St. John's. Grand times. Just down for a visit, are you?"

"Well, no," Bannister said. He had none of Miss Hiscock's reticence about putting forth the cover story; he would represent himself as a Zulu chieftain if necessary and stick to it in the face of any opposition. He spoke convincingly of the public meeting announcements and the survey being conducted to see if people had received and read them.

"Oh, yes," the other replied. "I got that in the mail. That's a grand thing. A grand thing. That'll be the making of us, the Offshore. Work for Mogul Oil, do you?"

"Well, no," Bannister said again. He explained about HIPE (Canada) and its consulting role. The storekeeper listened avidly, as though he had never heard anything half so interesting.

"Consulting, eh? Oh, it's a marvel altogether what they does these days. All that machinery." He shook his head in admiration. "I'm right glad it's gettin' on the go again— the Offshore, I mean. We needs something like that. What's your job with this...consulting?"

Bannister was beginning to be disconcerted by the man's tendency to slip uncomfortably direct questions in among his expressions of enthusiasm. However, since with any luck he hoped to be around for a while, he could see no convenient way of telling anything but the truth.

"Manager! And down here from the States! And here you've come all the way out to Parsons Arm to see how we're getting on! Well, that's grand. A great thing!" When it was put that way, Bannister began to feel that his cover story had certain weaknesses, but he could detect nothing in the shopkeeper's manner that hinted at anything but an honest, naive interest.

"Look here, now," the man said. "I'm pure delighted to see you here, and that's the fact. Why don't you step into the kitchen, look, and sit down for a minute? Maybe have a cup of tea? My name's Bishop, by the way, like it says on the sign. J.A. Bishop, he was my grandfather. My name's Theodore. Mostly, somebody with that name, they'd call him Ted, but they calls me The'. The' Bishop, see? It's a bit of a joke."

There seemed no way out. Bannister chuckled dutifully and introduced himself, using his given name of Ed, and allowed himself to be ushered into a back room while Bishop called out to his wife to take over behind the counter. In the flurry of introducing her to his guest and showing Bannister into the back room he took a moment to whisper to her urgently. "Give John a call. Tell him to get over here quick. And tell him not to let on why he come."

A second later he was in the kitchen pulling out a chair for Bannister and running on with effusive welcoming chatter.

"Now, then, Ed," he said, "I'm pure delighted to have a chance to talk with you. I'm that excited about all this offshore stuff.... Look, now, how about a cup of tea?" He turned to the stove, then appeared to change his mind. "No. I'll tell you what. This is a big day for Parsons Arm. Why don't we have a drop of something else?"

Bishop reached into a cupboard, brought out a bottle, banged it down on the table with a pair of large glasses, took the lid off with a flourish and sat down opposite Bannister.

"There, now. Pour yourself a drop of that." He beamed expectantly. "That's the way we does it in Newfoundland. I remembers the Ya...the Americans used to remark on it. 'Put out the bottle and every man for himself,' they'd say!"

Bannister, as he had told Al not so long ago, was not much of a drinker, but having come this far it would seem discourteous not to accept the hospitality so generously offered. He took the bottle and poured a small measure into his glass.

"Sure, that's not enough to wet your lips!" Bishop cried. "Go on, sir, take yourself a real swally!" Bannister obediently tilted the bottle again, this time splashing out rather more of the pale brown, faintly cloudy fluid than he had intended.

"That's more like it," Bishop said, pouring himself a half a tumbler. "I daresay you'll want a Coke with that. That's what the Americans liked in the war, God love them, rum and Coke. Why, I learned how to drink with the Americans, and me only fifteen!

"Shirl!" he shouted into the shop to his wife. "Bring us a couple of Cokes, will you?"

Bannister had not managed to eat much of a breakfast, and that had been several hours earlier; he appreciated the jolt of sweetness the Coca Cola provided. There was also a strange but not unpleasant aftertaste and a delayed-action glowing sensation as the first sip went down. Bishop had called it rum, and the label on the bottle seemed to support him, but in fact they were drinking a mixture of the storekeeper's own devising. About a quarter of it was indeed legally purchased Big Dipper, but the bottle had been topped up with clear grain alcohol brought in from St. Pierre. Its faintly cloudy appearance came from being topped up a second time with a generous measure of moonshine that Uncle Bob Crocker had given in lieu of a cash payment on his grocery bill. All things considered, it was a sly and dangerous mixture.

"Yes, sir," Bishop said after a generous draft, "I'm really lookin' forward to all this development. We needs it bad, I can tell you. But the thing is, Ed,"— and here his tone became confidential— "the thing of it is, we've got a special problem here in Parsons Arm.

"You see, pretty much the whole of The Shore, here, is R.C., and Parsons Arm is Church of England. Always has been and, God willin', always will be. Now, I don't want you to take me wrong. There's no bad feeling. There was, at one time, but that's all behind us now, thanks be to God. We gets along just fine now.

"But you can see how it is," he went on. "With all the rest of the communities R.C., and the Member R.C., and the Development Association pretty well all R.C.— well, sometimes Parsons Arm gets overlooked. Now, I ain't complainin'. It's only human nature for people to look out for their own."

None of this was leading Bannister any further with his search, but he was finding it pleasant for the moment to sit here in the kitchen while Bishop rambled on, and he was picking up possibly useful information. He sipped at his drink. He had become accustomed to the strange aftertaste, and he felt that the sweetness was giving his blood sugar a lift.

"Here, now," Bishop said, producing the Mogul Oil information kit. "This meeting you're checkin' up on. Look at the list, there, of the people takin' part. Nobody there from Parsons Arm.

"Now, you take...," he was beginning on a new theme as the back door opened to admit a tall, thin man in greasy coveralls.

"Mornin', T'e," the man said, "I come as soon as...."

"John!" Bishop broke in. "Ain't it lucky you dropped in!"

John looked uncertain. "Shirl said...."

Bishop cut him off again. "Never mind Shirl. She's lookin' after the shop. I'm glad you dropped in, John, because we've got an important visitor here. Ed, this is my brother-in-law, John Ellis, Shirl's brother." He produced another tumbler. "Calls for another drink, I'd say! There you are, Ed, give yourself a good one!"

Once they were settled again, Bishop took up where he had left off. "I was just tellin' Ed how things are here in The Arm. You take this little park we've been tryin' to get built. Just a playin' field for the kids. Now, you'd think that'd be the simplest thing in the world, wouldn't you? Well, sir, we've been workin' on that for so long you wouldn't believe it. Writin' to St. John's and applyin' for this and that...."

Bannister knew he should be out tracking down the missing documents, but it was comfortable and somehow reassuring to sit with these simple, friendly people, so caught up in their own small concerns. Besides, Bishop might be someone he could use later on, with his enthusiasm for development. He sipped and nodded.

"A playground for the kids doesn't seem like much," he said sympathetically. Bishop urged him to pour himself another.

As the conversation went on, Bannister felt more and more friendly toward his hosts. They certainly seemed to be struggling against some pretty heavy odds. He admired their enterprise, and told them so. Then, in case they had not understood, he told them again. Finally, as Bishop was encouraging him to pour himself just one more, a warning bell tinkled in the back of his mind. He wasn't quite sure what he had just been saying, but in any case it was time he got on with the job. He asked Bishop's advice about how best to proceed with his canvass of the community.

Bishop responded with the same enthusiasm he had shown for everything else. "Yes, indeed! I could sit here yarnin' all day, but you got work to do! I'd say you'd best start with Uncle Bob Crocker. He's the only other house on this side of the road, down by the water. Then you can go up the hill, there, to my sister's place...." He ushered Bannister out through the shop. "I'm delighted to have met you, Ed, and that's the fact. You drop in again any time...."

As Bannister went down the steps, walking carefully, Bishop darted back into the kitchen, where his brother-in-law was about to pour himself another drink.

"Seems like a nice fella," John said. "Not much of a drinker, though, I'd say." Bishop took the bottle from his hand and put it away. John looked hurt.

Bishop was peering out a side window, following Bannister's careful progress along the road. "Jeez, boy, T'e," John said. "I don't see why you sent him down to Uncle Bob's. Sure, the poor old bugger is deaf as the door. How's he going to...."

"I sent him down there," Bishop said, "to get him out of sight of his car for a few minutes. There, he's gone down the path. You get outside quick and fix his car so she won't go. Take out the rotor button or whatever they got on 'em these days. If that man drove back to St. John's in the state he's in, I'd never forgive myself."

John had learned long ago not to waste time questioning his brother-in-law at times like these. It saved argument. As he headed for the door, Bishop called him back and held out a bunch of keys. "After you fixes his car, just run mine around front and put it beside his."

John slipped out and was back quickly. "She won't go no place now," he said, and waited for the explanations he knew would come when The' was ready.

Bishop held out his hand for his keys. John looked blank for a moment and then understood. "Oh, I left 'em. Habit, I guess. Workin' on cars all the time...."

"No matter," said Bishop. "Now, when he comes back and his car won't start, I'll call you to have a look at her. You tell him...tell him whatever you like, only make sure he knows you can't get her runnin' right away. Then you and me will run him into town in mine, and we'll tell him we'll bring his in to him as soon as you've got her fixed. Understand?" John nodded.

"Good. Now, another thing. When we takes his car back you don't accept nothin' for fixin' her. Just a friendly gesture. Got that?" John nodded again, more reluctantly.

"Good," said Bishop. "Now, this is important. Tomorrow mornin', first thing, I wants you to get Mabel to call up Very Low...."

"Jeez, boy," John broke in with a nervous look over his shoulder toward the door to the shop, "not so loud!"

Bishop had been referring to a popular phone-in radio programme where callers from across the province aired their grievances each week-day morning while the abrasive host, Gerry Snow, urged them on. Mr. Snow's many fans, mostly women, would not stand for the disparaging nickname used by his equally numerous and mostly male detractors.

"You let Shirl or Mabel hear you call him that," John whispered, "and...."

"I'll call him anything I likes," said Bishop, but John noticed that he, too, had dropped his voice and glanced apprehensively toward the shop.

"Anyway, all I wants her to say," Bishop went on, "is that she heard some place that one of them big oil outfits is going to build a playground in Parsons Arm, and does anybody know anything about it. That's all. If nobody takes it up, I'll get Shirl or some of the other women to call in later. All right? You can remember that?"

."Jeez," John said, his brow wrinkling in concentration. "Did that fella say that? I never heard...."

"You just leave the listenin' to me, John, boy, because I'm better at it. You heard him say he'd do anything he could to help us, didn't you? You heard that?"

"Oh, he said that all right. About six times. I never seen a man get so friendly on three or four drinks."

"All right, then. Now, them oil companies have got all kinds of money, and they're lashin' it out all the time. Ain't that so?"

"Well, yes. I expect...."

"And this fella's the manager of one of them?"

"So he says...."

"...And the manager is the fella that gives the orders?"

John nodded.

"Well, there you are. If you're talkin' about something that costs some money, and if the boss of some outfit that's got a lot of money tells you he'll do anything in his power to help you, then what does that add up to?"

"Oh," said John. "Never thought of it that way. I expects you're right." He shook his head admiringly. "That's nice of him, ain't it? But what's all this stuff about phonin' to talk about it on the radio?"

"I just wants him to remember as good as we do," Bishop said.

Bannister picked his way down the path. His feet seemed to be unaccountably far away, and he was finding that he had to concentrate on every movement.

At the end of the path a bank fell away sharply to a gravel beach about six feet below. Uncle Bob Crocker's house, an old fish shed that he had converted to a two-room bachelor cabin, stood on pilings which brought its floor about level with the end of the path. A pair of planks spanned the gap, leading from the top of the bank to a narrow gallery that ran along the side of the little house. On the gallery, in front of the door, Uncle Bob's two elderly dogs lay in a hairy tangle, wheezing and twitching in their sleep.

Placing his feet with care, Bannister stepped out on the bridge of planks. The dogs, with an air of performing a necessary but tiresome duty, struggled arthritically to their feet and tumbled along the gallery toward him, barking hoarsely in welcome. Taken off guard, Bannister lurched, clutched despairingly for a non-existent handrail, toppled sideways into the gap between the house and the bank, and disappeared into a rank tangle of bushes and weeds.

His sudden departure was almost as great a surprise to the dogs as it was to Bannister. They milled about in confusion, peering mistily into the shadows below the house, sniffing and uttering inquiring whines. They had done what they were supposed to do, and were quite willing to greet the visitor. But they could hardly be expected, at their time of life, to go leaping down onto the beach after him. They panted and woofed and wagged their tails, inviting him to give up his foolishness and come across the bridge properly.

Uncle Bob had not heard the commotion— indeed, he had not heard much of anything for thirty years— but the dogs' lumbering movements shook the little house and attracted his attention. He slammed open the door, and seeing only the dogs, roared at them good-naturedly.

"Har, ye buggers!" he bellowed. "Cats! Sic 'em! Huss! Huss!" and hurled the door shut again with a report that echoed across the cove.

Most people judge the force that they put into everyday movements at least partly by sound; people who can't hear are guided in a large measure by the reactions of people around them. Being deaf and living alone, Uncle Bob Crocker had no guide at all. He went about his daily activities with a cheerful vigour, accompanied by a fearful clattering of stove lids, crashing of crockery, and banging of cupboard doors. His neighbours often remarked that if anybody were to live with him for any length of time, they would soon be as deaf as he was.

At the moment he was thumping and crashing about his little kitchen-cum-living room preparing mid-day dinner for himself and the dogs, adding to all the other noises the one sound he could faintly hear: his own foghorn voice delivering one of his favourite hymns at a volume that would do credit to a lead singer in a rock band.

Below the house, Bannister was slowly sorting himself out, impeded by the stunning effects of his fall, the alcohol he had consumed, and the scratchy tangle of bushes. He tested his limbs with great caution, wishing he were back in Texas and had a gun. Clearly, he was in imminent danger from a mad old hermit who had first set his dogs on him and was now smashing about and bellowing in the house above in some sort of lunatic frenzy, undoubtedly working up to a new attack.

Slowly and painfully, Bannister crawled beneath the little house between the pilings that supported it, over slimy, evil-smelling rocks toward the water, where he hoped to make his escape along the beach. He reached the edge of the house and crouched there, below a window, looking warily around for the dogs.

"EETERRRNAAL FAADER, STRONG TO SAAAVE...!" Uncle Bob roared in a window-rattling monotone. He turned to the stove and picked up a pot that was bubbling aromatically there, containing a lump of his own salt fish, a couple of potatoes, and a few chunks of turnip.

"OHHH, HEAR US WHEN WE CRIES TO DEEEE...." He slammed open the window overlooking the water.

"...FOR DOSE IN PERRRILLL ON...." Holding the pot in one hand and the lid with the other, he drained the scalding liquid out the window and turned to put his dinner on the table.

He did not, of course, hear the outraged cry from Bannister, below the window. The dogs did, however, and they lumbered resignedly to their feet again and barked half-heartedly as Bannister shot around the corner of the little house and plunged straight up the bank through the bushes, trailing curses and wisps of savory steam.

"From the smell of it," one of the dogs said, "that fella's made off with our dinner."

"Let 'im," said the other. "'Tis only old salt fish and turnip again, anyway."

"But shouldn't we charge after 'im, just for the look of the thing?"

"You can if you wants to, but you'll only make yourself look foolish. That fella's too athletic for us altogether—crawlin' around under the house, and crashin' through them bushes like that. He'd run us to death for nothin'."

"You're right," said the first dog. "Shag 'im." And they lay down again in front of the door.

Bannister ploughed straight up the nearly perpendicular bank through the bushes and burst out onto the road where he paused for a moment to wipe at the stinging, gummy fluid that dripped into his eyes, and look apprehensively behind to see if he was being pursued. When his vision cleared a little, he sprinted the few hundred feet back to the store. He wrenched open the car door, fumbled for a moment with the keys, and roared away up the hill out of town, leaving two black tire marks on the road and a stench of burning rubber in the air.

The' and John stood on the porch of the store in awed silence, listening to the diminishing sound of the engine. It was the first time in his life that John could remember his brother-in-law having nothing to say.

On the road outside the town Constable Wasylenchuk, late of Winnipeg, and Constable Cameron, late of Glace Bay, and both late of the RCMP training barracks in Regina, were approaching Parsons Arm when The' Bishop's car shot past them in the opposite direction, driven at extremely high speed by a wild-looking person who was clearly not Bishop. Wasylenchuk wheeled the cruiser around and gave chase while Cameron started the siren and lights and lifted the radio mike to report to headquarters.

Shortly after, the police car drew up in front of the store in Parsons Arm with Bannister slumped dejectedly in the rear. Bishop's car followed a few minutes later driven by Constable Cameron, who had taken time to cover the wet and smelly front seat with a sheet of plastic intended for transporting bodies that were bleeding or incontinent.

The ensuing discussion was long and complicated. Bannister's attempts to account for himself were barely coherent. When Uncle Bob Crocker was summoned and saw the policemen he promptly and loudly denied any knowledge of an unlicensed moose, pieces of which were lying neatly wrapped in several household freezers in the town. The Mounties made every effort to relate a moose to the events they were investigating, but since the person who had introduced the subject insisted he knew nothing about it, their efforts had little effect.

Constable Wasylenchuk, to be on the safe side, advised everybody that anything they said would be taken down in writing and might be used in evidence against them, but the more he scribbled in his notebook statements concerning moose, boiling poisonous material being poured from windows, savage dogs, and house-to-house surveys on oil development, the less he felt that he would want to quote any of it in court.

In the end, the only solid piece of evidence they had was Bannister himself, whom they had apprehended while in care and control of a motor vehicle, and who was clearly in a condition of impairment. He was all they had to show for the time and energy they had invested, and they were not about to let go of him. In spite of his increasingly profane protestation, they finally drove away with him still in the back seat of the police car. "My Jeez," said John. "I'm glad you called me over, T'e. Wouldn't want to have missed that, whatever it was." He furrowed his brow in concentration. "But I don't quite see where the moose comes into it."

"Just forget about the shaggin' moose," said Bishop, poking irritably at the wet spots on the seat of his car. "You know anything that's good for cleanin' upholstery?"

"I don't expect that fella will be givin' us no playing field now," John suggested.

"It's a set-back," Bishop said. "No question about that. Still, you never knows. We might be able to make use of it some way. We'll take him back his car, anyhow, a bit later on. I expect the Mounties will be able to tell us where he lives. And we might as well go ahead with the radio tomorrow morning. You never knows, and that's the fact."

"NICE YOUNG FELLAS, THEM MOUNTIES," Uncle Bob bellowed conversationally. "I WONDER WHO THE OTHER ONE WAS? NEVER SEEN HIM AROUND BEFORE."

Bishop gave him a disgusted look before going back into his store.

IX

Bannister sat behind his desk and glowered at the door. The right half of his face shone an angry red and glistened with burn ointment, accentuating twenty-four hours' growth of beard stubble. The scalp on that side was too tender for more than token grooming, so the hair was wild and matted. A slit of bloodshot eye peered evilly from behind a puffy, swollen lid. By contrast, the washed, shaved and combed left side of his head seemed pale and gaunt and almost spiritual, like a martyred saint in a painting. The left half gave off the scent of expensive aftershave, while the right emitted a strange, mingled, hospital cafeteria odour of antiseptic, fish and boiled turnip. All things considered he looked, and perhaps even smelled, rather like Dr. Jekyll in the process of turning into Mr. Hyde.

Reviewing the experiences of the previous day, he alternated between fantasies of hideous revenge and desperate brainstorming of new ideas for retrieving the plans. He had to admit to himself that on the whole he had not handled the policemen very well. What had seemed at the time to be devastatingly witty remarks about King of the Royal Mounted, dog teams, and the prominent yellow stripe down the Mounties' trouser legs now appeared, in the dyspeptic light of morning, to have been ill-advised.

Even at that, the constables had not immediately laid any formal charges. After dropping off his partner, Constable Wasylenchuk had taken Bannister to the clinic in St. Cyril's for treatment of his burns and scratches. If it had not been for that, things might have been different.

Bannister and the policeman were not the only customers in the tiny emergency department. In a corner, a slim, attractive, brown-skinned young woman in a lab coat was attempting to administer a tetanus shot to a squalling, struggling, red-faced child. She had already sustained a sharp kick just below the knee, and was proceeding with caution. In another corner the little boy's mother and aunt were deep in serious discussion of the relative chances of winning the jackpot in various lotteries, apparently oblivious to the conflict. Constable Wasylenchuk picked up a magazine and Bannister, exhausted by recent events and already beginning to regret some of the things he had said in the police car, blearily watched as the small medical drama unfolded.

"Oh, my goodness, you should not cry so!" the young woman said soothingly, trying without success to manoeuvre her hypodermic close to one of the flailing little arms. Her accent sounded Arabic to Bannister, and made him think with a rush of nostalgia of Bahrain and Saudi Arabia.

"You should be brave. Like a big fishing man, perhaps, or something like that." She dodged another kick and raised the needle. "Look. It is only a small, little prick...."

In an instant the two other women were on their feet and one of them— presumably the mother— had snatched up the bawling youngster.

"You got no right to talk to him like that!" she shouted. "Poor little fella!" She hugged the child fiercely, stifling his cries against her bosom so that her last words echoed jarringly in the sudden silence.

"But I have said nothing...," the brown-skinned girl protested, astonished.

"Maybe you calls it nuttin'," said the child's aunt, "but let me tell you, we don't stand for usin' language the like of that to a poor innocent child! We heard what you called him!"

"But I do not understand...."

"Oh, yes," said the mother. "These nurses! They pretends they don't understand ordinary English, but they knows them kind of words, all right. I wants to see the doctor!" she demanded.

"Against the law, that kind of language is," the other woman said. "Exceptin' in the movies." She wheeled on Constable Wasylenchuk. "Ain't that so? Ain't it against the law?"

Wasylenchuk explained mildly that he had been reading, and had not heard anything illegal.

Bannister, however, had heard everything, and *felt* it with a preternatural clarity. It seemed to him that the incident summed up in poignant microcosm all the misunderstandings and hostilities of the human condition. He felt uplifted by a blaze of insight which, if he would only express it, could bring peace and harmony between black and white, between rich and poor, third world and first, oil developers and natives.

He tried to explain, first offering a polite greeting in Arabic to the brown-skinned young woman, who was looking in open-mouthed bewilderment from one to another and appeared to be about to cry. It was not an easy idea to get across, and was made even more difficult by the fact that his own voice seemed to be coming from somewhere about three feet behind his head, but it was important, and he did his best.

The aunt crossed her arms and looked Bannister up and down. "Oh," she said. "So now we're going to get a sermon from some shaggin' old drunk!" She turned a penetrating glare on Constable Wasylenchuk. "Would you tell me," she said, "— buddy-boy here, who looks like he's threw up down his clothes— is he under arrest, or what?"

Looking back, it seemed to Bannister that this had been the turning point. Wasylenchuk considered the two irate women, the child who after being nearly smothered in his mother's protective embrace had now fought free and was shrieking louder than ever in near hysterics, and the appalled young woman still holding her hypodermic needle, and seemed to hold Bannister somehow responsible for it all.

"Yes," he said.

"Right," said the aunt. "Then maybe you'll be so good as to tell him to keep his shaggin' nose out of things that doesn't concern him. Especially seein' as it seems we can't look for no help from the shaggin' RCMP when our own flesh and blood is bein' called all kinds of dirty names right in front of us by all kinds of foreigners!"

"We wants to see the doctor!" the child's mother repeated.

"Yes," said the aunt, "for a start. But that won't be the whole of it, not by a long stretch. I wants a phone. I'm callin' the Minister of Health. And Mr. Merrigan. And whoever's in charge of them so-called police." She jerked her head contemptuously at Wasylenchuk. "And tomorrow mornin'," she finished triumphantly, "I'm callin' Gerry Snow on the Open Phone!"

The young woman put down her hypodermic syringe and slipped out of the room, returning after a moment in the protective shadow of a stout, grey-haired nurse who immediately set about restoring order. The two women who had been so voluble a moment before shrank visibly in her presence, and listened meekly when she explained that they could just give up demanding to see the doctor, because the young woman they were shouting at *was* the doctor. They could also give up screeching and bawling about bad language, because didn't everybody know that the two of them, together or singly, had been able to out-curse any five men on The Shore since before they'd been able to wipe their own...noses, not that she believed for a minute that the doctor had used any bad language, though if she did who could blame her seeing the sort of thing she had to put up with. And as for young Timmy, if he would be a good little love and stop his noise he would not get the clip on the ear he so richly deserved, but could have this nice big peppermint knob, and if he'd take his shot like a man he could have two more like it to put in his pocket. And Bannister, for his part, could just give up jabbering at Dr. Mahalingam in whatever foreign language he was going on in, because she couldn't understand him any better than anybody else, and it was making her upset, poor dear, and didn't she have enough trouble already.

In the course of her explanations, she administered young Timmy's shot, rinsed Bannister's head under the sink, applied medication to his burns and scratches, and sent Dr. Mahalingam off to lie down for a while with a cold compress on her forehead.

Bannister could see that she was the sort of person who would be able to grasp his insight into the human condition, and while she ministered to his wounds he told her about it. At the time, he felt that she understood. At least partly. "That's right, my duck," she had said, patting his cheek. "And next time try to get some of your dinner inside of you instead of all over your head." Through it all, Constable Wasylenchuk said nothing. He took Bannister to the RCMP headquarters, inspected his driver's licence and identification, and laid formal charges of dangerous and impaired driving before taking him back to St. John's.

As he sat behind his desk next morning, Bannister cringed with embarrassment when he thought of his attempts to explain how the world could live in harmony, but it was the charges that really preyed on his mind. If Al got wind of that— and Jarvis was certain to see that he would— things could be even more uncomfortable than they already were. He had to find some way to get the charges dropped.

Miss Hiscock entered briskly five minutes before the appointed hour. Sensing his mood, she asked no questions, but made him coffee without being asked and then sat down across from him and wisely said nothing. They were meeting, as arranged, at seven a.m.

to compare notes on the previous day's beginning on the search for the missing papers. Theresa, feeling that her achievements warranted taking a few liberties, breezed in at ten past the hour.

"Hi, everybody," she said airily. "Sorry I'm a bit late. Jeez, what's that funny sme...."

She was cut off in mid-word by a meaningful glance from Miss Hiscock. It was not the usual schoolmistress frown, but rather a direct, almost telepathic warning from one woman to another in the presence of a man in a dangerous frame of mind. It was also the first piece of straightforward communication that had ever passed between them, person-to-person, unencumbered by considerations of class, age, or status. Both were subliminally aware of this, and filed it away for future analysis. Theresa sat down quickly and assumed a demure and deferential posture.

"All right," Bannister began, twisting a paper clip savagely and wincing from the pain of a sprained wrist. He outlined his adventures in Parsons Arm, dwelling on the insane malice of Uncle Bob Crocker, and leaving out any reference to the RCMP. "...So this goddamn door to door stuff isn't going to work," he concluded. "We need another strategy."

Theresa was dismayed. She had thoroughly enjoyed her day and was looking forward to more like it. Indeed, she had developed several plans for extending the campaign as long as possible. She was searching for something that might change Bannister's mind when help came from a most unexpected quarter.

"Perhaps you are being a little hasty, Mr. Bannister," Miss Hiscock said. "I can see that you have had a very nasty experience, but we haven't heard yet how Theresa got along. And for my part, I believe I have made a most valuable contact." For some reason her cheeks felt as hot as Bannister's right one looked, but she pressed on. "Perhaps Theresa and I should report first, and then you can consider...?"

They reported, seconding each other to such a degree that it might have been rehearsed. Theresa, of course, knew Mr. Callahan— everybody on the Shore knew Mr. Callahan— and she certainly agreed that his promise of cooperation with Miss Hiscock would almost guarantee a quick recovery of the papers. She had intended to leave any mention of Carm and Jackie and Phonse out of her own report, but drastic measures seemed to be called for. She said that some friends had drove her around, like, and instead of correcting her grammar Miss Hiscock praised her initiative and even, to Theresa's carefully disguised delight, made a suggestion that Theresa herself had wanted to make but didn't dare— that she be given some funds to continue the arrangement and reward her helpers.

Miss Hiscock, who seemed uncharacteristically to have taken over the role of chairperson, summed up. "It does appear as though Theresa and I have had some very good luck. Now, if I were to take advantage of Mr. Callahan's very kind offer of assistance, and Theresa and her young friends were to continue their efforts, I'm sure we will recover that kit before long. Perhaps, Mr. Bannister, you should go home for the day and have a good rest."

"I dunno," said Bannister despondently. The whole thing seemed to be slipping out of his control, but his head was hurting inside from Bishop's rum and outside from Uncle Bob's dinner. He had spent most of the night alternately throwing up and putting ointment on his face. It was very difficult to concentrate, and no better plan suggested itself.

"Okay," he said finally. "I guess we might as well try it. At least for another day. Until we can think of something else."

"Well, that's settled, then," Miss Hiscock said briskly. "We'll get started right away. I'll give Theresa a run down to The Shore, and go on and see Mr. Callahan. Can you call your friends, Theresa? Oh, yes, and how much shall we give her for her helpers? I'm sure there's enough in petty cash for today, and perhaps tomorrow...."

The two women bustled about the office in full cooperation, while Bannister went back to reflecting on his other problems. If he was back in Texas or almost any place else, it would be all right. In Saudi, of course, they locked people up for a year for drinking, even if they weren't driving, but in Saudi he'd know what strings to pull. In most places, as a last resort, he might even get some help from the CIA. But here....

A thought laboriously crossed his mind as the two women were about to go out the door, and he called Theresa back. "This Merrigan guy— this politician. You say his own staff says he's crooked?"

"Oh yes, Mr. Bannister," Theresa agreed eagerly, anxious to follow Miss Hiscock. "Everybody knows that. Crooked as a stick!"

"And you say he...ah...gets dirty with the girls in his office?"

Theresa giggled. "All the time. They're forever talking about it."

She clattered off down the stairs. Bannister swallowed three aspirins with a gulp of cold coffee, tipped back his swivel chair, put his feet up on the desk and leaned his head back carefully against the wall. I'll just take a bit of a rest, he thought, until nine. Then I guess I better set up an appointment. It'll probably cost an arm and a leg, but if I can get this old shyster to fix the impaired driving thing.... His eyes drooped shut.

He was awakened by a heavy tread on the stair outside. The sleep had done little good— his head still ached, and now his neck hurt, too. The door to his inner office was open, and he could see across the outer room to the hall door, with HIPE (Canada) on the glass, backwards from his perspective and looking like some alien script. He had time only to hope fervently that whoever it was would go on to the next floor, or at least that the door was locked, before both hopes were dashed.

The door swung open, and Pastor Jarvis stood in the opening. "Ah, good morning Bronco, my friend!" Jarvis's booming greeting set up painful echoes in

Bannister's head. "God bless you! It's a beautiful day...."

As he spoke, Jarvis was shooting a quick glance around the outer office. His demeanour changed in a flash. "The girls aren't here? Good. I want to talk to you." The toothy smile and the evangelical heartiness had vanished. He strode into the inner office and shut the door.

"Listen," Bannister began, "I don't want...."

"It doesn't much matter what you want." Jarvis flipped a chair into position to one side of the desk and sat where Bannister had to turn his stiff neck at an awkward angle to face him. "Are you aware that half this town is talking about some oil outfit that has lost some important papers?"

Bannister looked blank and took a sip of cold coffee to cover his surprise and alarm. How in hell could anybody have heard so soon?

"Most of them don't know which oil outfit it is, and they don't seem to know what the papers are. But some people also know that you and your two girls were running around the Hard Shore yesterday with some cock-and-bull story about those Mogul information kits."

Bannister's head throbbed faster with his increased heartbeat. "You're a real mine of information, aren't you?" he said nastily. "The boys in Virginia must be real proud of you."

Jarvis ignored the taunt, his pale eyes unblinking. "Well?" he said.

"Well what?

"I want an explanation, and I want it quick. That's what."

"*You* want an explanation? Who the hell do you think you are? The CIA isn't running this show. I am. You can go...."

"Bannister," Jarvis said with quiet menace. "Don't play games. You can run your little show, and you can screw it up— as you seem to be doing— to your heart's content. But when it's a matter of national security...."

"National security? What in hell are you talking about?" He was both panicky and incredulous. The preacher couldn't possibly know what was missing. Or could he?

Jarvis brought his hand down flat on the desk with a bang. "I said don't play games with me! You've got sensitive material in this office. Material bearing on the strategic interests of the United States of America. God knows why anybody would trust you with it, but you've got it.

"Now, when I hear that some incompetent drill-pusher out of Houston has let some papers go astray, and when I know that he's got papers that nobody in his right mind should have let him have in the first place, why, I begin to get a bit worried."

Bannister felt a slight relief. At least the CIA man didn't know the full extent of the disaster. "So go worry some place else. We don't take orders from you guys...."

"I'm going to give you about sixty seconds more," Jarvis said. "I want to see your Top Secret files, and I want to see all of them, and I want to see them now. If they're all there— and I know exactly what you've got in your little burn box— if everything is present and accounted for, then I'll go away and let you go on making a mess out of this job. That part is none of my concern. I don't care what you've lost as long as it isn't something that *is* my concern. Now, get out the files."

Bannister blustered a little more, and Jarvis stood up. "Okay," he said. "If that's the way you want it. I'm going home now, and I'm going to make a full report. I don't know why I didn't do it right away. I gave you your chance. You won't show me the files, but by tonight there'll be a few guys in here that you *will* show them to. You'd be surprised how many people in my organization would be glad of a chance to put you Houston johnnies in your place."

"You wouldn't do that." Bannister's voice lacked conviction, even in his own ears.

"Look, my friend, some of us don't think you people should be allowed to operate the way you do at all. You've got stuff in your files that could be very embarrassing to Washington, to say the least. Not the oil stuff— we don't care about that. If Mogul screws that up, one of the others will get it. But you've got material in there about highly sensitive political matters. Covert operations. Intervention in the affairs of a sovereign state. Why, there's even things that could be construed as plans for a military involvement, in certain circumstances. In the wrong hands, what you've got in your files could be dynamite."

"Yeah," said Bannister bitterly. "And who put it there? Not us. It's you goddamn CIA bird-dogs that insist on sticking that stuff in. You and your goddamn scenarios," he sneered. "If it wasn't for that...."

Jarvis sank back into his chair, looking suddenly stricken. "Jesus!" he said. It was the first time Bannister had seen his cover slip, but he hardly noticed. "When I came here this morning I thought this was just a routine check. You'd show me the files were safe and that'd be it. But I'm beginning to think you really have lost something hot!" He looked intently at Bannister for a moment. "You *have*, haven't you?" he said in an awed near-whisper.

Bannister's survival instincts were beginning to come to full alert. He had been badly shaken to hear that Jarvis already knew part of his secret, but now he caught the note of panic in the other's voice and his mind began to work again. "You may never know, Reverend," he said. "But just suppose I had. Just suppose the whole goddamn Master Plan was out there some place like a bomb waiting to go off. I'm not saying it is, but just suppose." He stood up and walked to the window overlooking Duckworth Street.

"You're right, you know," he went on conversationally. "There's a lot of crazy stuff in those files. And a lot of it ain't the kind of thing an oil company would be bothered with. Seems to me that if the wrong people got a look at it they wouldn't have much trouble tracing it back to you.

"And I guess we both know how your outfit operates. You get a leak like that, and they don't care much who was responsible as long as they can cover their ass."

He was beginning to get into his stride. "I wonder how they'd do it," he mused. "I suppose they could set us both up as a pair of crackpot super-patriots or something, out here cooking up fantastic schemes on our own. Or maybe KGB plants trying to stir up trouble between the U.S. of A. and her good neighbour, Canada. Something like that. Probably make us out to be fags, too. A couple of middle-aged homos blackmailed by the Russkies. That usually works pretty good with preachers." Jarvis said nothing. The interview was not going at all the way he had expected.

Bannister lit a cigarette and looked thoughtfully at the rising smoke. "Of course, your guys don't like to leave too much to chance. And it's a lot easier to lay something like that on somebody who ain't around to defend themselves. It wouldn't be the first time a couple of patsies in our position got involved in a serious accident or a nice, neat murder-suicide, would it?"

Jarvis finally found his voice. "You stupid bastard! You...."

"My, my! Such language from a man of God." The paper on his cigarette had become wet with the ointment on his fingers, and he stubbed it out. "Well, Reverend, you just go call Virginia and get things started. I think I'll go home to bed." With nothing left to lose, he felt nearly as calm as he sounded.

"All right," Jarvis said, his face pale and tight. "How bad is it? Did you really lose the Master Plan? How in the name of...never mind. I don't want to know. The thing is, can we get it back?"

"That's better, Reverend," Bannister said. "A lot better. Only there's a couple of little things we need to get straight. First of all, I didn't say I'd lost the Master Plan, I just said *suppose*. Like for instance. Okay, maybe I have lost something, but you don't know what it is, and as far as I'm concerned you ain't going to know.

"Second, you talk about *us* getting it back. Only it occurs to me that if it really was something important, and if you got to it first, you might think about letting Virginia in on it anyway, once you're in the clear." The pastor's expression showed that the thought had crossed his mind. "So, it ain't *us* that's going to get it back. It's *me*. Understand?"

"Look, my friend, there's no need for all this hostility." Jarvis was trying hard to assume his usual unctuous parson's voice. "All I'm interested in is protecting the interests of the country we both...."

"Yeah. Right. And I'm interested in protecting my back. Now, I admit I've got a bit of a problem here. If you'd kept your goddamn nose out of it, I'd have dealt with it myself. But now that you've stuck your nose in, you can help."

"Certainly, Bronco. Certainly. I can call on resources...."

"Never mind the resources. This is between you and me, and I want it to stay that way. You're going to stay right out of the field, understand?"

"For heaven's sake, man, be reasonable. How can I help if I can't put people in the field?"

"You can help with strategy and information. We need to keep the lid on this...."

"Keep the lid on?" Jarvis gave a mirthless laugh. "With half the town talking about it?"

"You said yourself they don't know what it is, or who. We're going to keep it that way. You can use your goddamn resources to keep tab on the talk in the city, spread counter-rumours when we need to...oh, there's plenty you can do. But if I get the slightest hint that you're trying to get to those papers first.... Well, I know more than enough to put you right in the middle of any shit-storm. If I go down, you'll come with me. Got it?" The preacher gave an exasperated snort but said nothing. "Okay. Now maybe we can talk some cooperation. Want a cup of coffee?"

They were deep in planning when the outer office door opened and Schultz's voice called, "Bronco? Anybody here?"

"In here, Schultz," Bannister said. "What do you want?"

Schultz caught sight of Jarvis. "Oh, hello, Reverend. Nice day. Listen Bannister, I need to talk to you.... My God, what happened to your face? And what's that funny smell in here? Smells like...." Bannister's expression stopped him. "Yeah," he said. "Well, listen. I've got to talk to you." He flicked his eyes sideways toward Jarvis.

"It's all right, Schultz," Bannister said. "You can talk in front of the Pastor."

"But...."

"I said it's all right. He's my...ah...spiritual advisor, you might say. We have no secrets from each other. Or not as many as I'd like."

"Oh," said Schultz uncertainly. "Yeah. Well, I got two things. First of all, there's a rumour going around about some oil outfit that's lost some papers. Most people think it's us. You know anything about that?"

"Yes," said Bannister. "Now, what else?"

Schultz looked even more uncertain. "Well, the other thing is, that radio open-line guy they call Very Low's got all kinds of people calling up and blabbing about some oil company that's promised to build a playground or something in Parsons Arm. Most people seem to thing that's us, too. Our switchboard is jammed with people from every other community on the Hard Shore wanting to know why they aren't getting one. Only I've been doing a bit of checking, and it sounds to me like the guy who's been promising playgrounds is probably you."

The victory over Jarvis had buoyed up Bannister's spirits a little, but suddenly his headache was back and he felt ill and tired again.

"I don't know what in hell...excuse me, Reverend... I don't know what you think you're doing," Schultz went on, "but that kind of thing is very bad public rel...community liaison. You can't go promising something to one of these places, and not the others. And everybody thinks it's us." He looked at Bannister accusingly.

"Just sit down a minute, Schultz," Bannister said heavily. "We got something to tell you." He turned to Jarvis. "Looks like we got another partner, Reverend."

Schultz heard the story in astonishment and rising consternation. "You mean the whole Master Plan? Out there? In one of our kits?"

"Could be," Bannister said. "There's something out there, and the Pastor seems to think that's what it is. I'm the only one who knows for sure, but I ain't talking. However, seems to me that if there is any kind of secret stuff out there, Mogul ain't going to be very pleased. It also seems to me that they ain't going to give much of a damn how it got there, are they? You're the guy responsible for the kits, right? I'd say that if they have to start covering their ass, they're going to use you to do it, Schultzie. What do you think?"

"Oh, God," said Schultz.

"Amen," said Jarvis. "Which brings us back to the matter in hand. The longer that paper is loose the less chance we have of ever getting it back. We need some quick action. Now, most of the people on the Hard Shore are Catholics...."

"Except for Parsons Arm," Schultz interjected, ever the local expert.

"Except for Parsons Arm. The parish priest is named Morrissey, a liberal-leftie who's always dabbling in politics and protest movements, and development things...."

"Anti-development, you mean," said Schultz. "Until a few minutes ago I thought he was going to be our biggest problem out there."

113

"He could be yet," Jarvis said. "If somebody finds something funny in his information kit, there's a pretty good chance he'd talk to Morrissey about it. Catholics are like that. Always run to the priest with anything they don't understand."

"How about your little flock, Reverend?" Bannister said. "Don't they take you into their confidence? Maybe they don't trust you."

"Shut up, Bannister. I don't like you any better than you like me, but we can leave that for later. We've got to get on top of this fast. The first thing we can do is find out whether Morrissey knows anything yet. You two can do it—just a general discussion about potential oil development. If he's heard anything, he's bound to drop a clue or two. Okay?"

No one had explained Jarvis's role to Schultz, but he was beginning to put enough pieces together to realize that he would prefer not to have it spelled out for him. He agreed meekly.

"All right," Jarvis said. "Now, what else?"

X

Chief Engineering Officer Mitsuru Oshawara awoke early and noted with a pleasant sense of anticipation that the porthole across from his bunk framed a circle of brilliant blue sky, confirming the previous night's meteorological report. He got up quickly, showered, and dressed in his hiking clothes, not forgetting to lay out a warm sweater, cap, and jacket, since the reports had forecast bright skies but chilly winds. His anticipation increased as he left his cabin for breakfast.

His ship, the *Ashika Maru*, lay beside the apron in St. John's harbour, the sun gleaming almost painfully from the surgical white of her paint. To her stern, in vivid contrast, two dowdy Portuguese trawlers wallowed companionably side by side, great streaks of rust all but obscuring their once green and white sides, their afterdecks a cheerful jumble of buoys, barrels, rope, and odd bits of equipment, and their lower rigging decorated with a multi-coloured line of washing.

The city was just waking up. A few cars moved by on the road beside the apron, a winch began to growl on a big Russian factory ship across the harbour by the oil docks, and two dishevelled women picked their way down the gangplank of the inboard Portuguese vessel, teetering on high heels and calling raucous farewells over their shoulders to a pair of seamen yawning and grinning on the deck.

Back in his cabin after breakfast and a quick inspection tour of the engine room, Oshawara assembled his equipment— a lunch neatly packed by the ship's cook, cameras, lenses, film, tripod, binoculars, notebook. The *Ashika Maru* had been in St. John's for two days, loading frozen squid. Today would be a slack day. There was some delay, as usual, and no trucks would be arriving until late afternoon at the earliest. All the routine work in his department was well in hand and Oshawara was going to spend this little gift of free time pursuing his hobby, photographing landscapes and, where possible, wildlife.

He had some difficulty making himself understood at the car rental agency, and he could not make out most of what the clerk there said to him, apart from the prices, which were written down anyway, but it all worked out. His International Driving Permit and American Express Card bridged the communication gap and soon he was rolling out of the city in a Toyota very similar to the one in his garage back home, though this one was rather more spartan and not nearly as well maintained. It was delightful to get away from the ship for a while.

From the map folded on the passenger seat he picked a road that looped intriguingly along the coast, and spent an absorbing morning collecting a series of photographs of stunted, dark evergreen forests, looming cliffs, and stretches of barren bog. The landscape was rather too wild, undisciplined, and empty for his taste and the occasional village too alien, but if some of the compositions came off, he would have a most interesting series to add to his collection.

He ate his lunch in deep contentment on a rocky hill above a raggedly sprawling town a little larger than most of the hamlets he had passed during the morning. Not much activity was visible, but he noticed three men emerge from a house next to a large, white wooden building with a pointed tower. A temple, presumably— or, no, the English word was *church*. A little self-consciously, he tried pronouncing it. It had an odd, awkward sound. Two of the men got into an automobile and drove away. The third, all in black, stood watching them for a moment, doing something with his hands that Oshawara could not make out, then appeared to light a cigarette. After a moment the black-clad figure began to walk slowly toward the hill. Oh hell, Oshawara thought. I hope he doesn't come up here.

It was not that he was particularly shy, or did not want to meet the local people. Far from it. He would have liked nothing better than to be able to wander through their strange little villages and talk with them. The trouble was that Chief Engineering Officer Mitsuru Oshawara had, much to his regret, no facility at all with languages. He had managed, just barely, to pass his English exams at technical college. He could read it reasonably well, as long as what he was reading was on a technical subject. Unfortunately, though, dynamos and condensers and valve-couplings do not turn up very often in casual conversation.

Not that it would make much difference if they did, because try as he might, Oshawara could not seem to guide his tongue through the jungle of consonants that make up so many English words. Even when he could think of the right thing to say, he usually could not pronounce it so that others could recognize it. Back in his cabin he had a box of tape cassettes prepared by an anglophilic Tokyo language teacher on which the voice of a moonlighting BBC television actor rolled out useful sentences, with a pause between for the student to repeat them. The more expert speakers of English among his shipmates said the accent was all wrong: American was the thing to learn, they told him. But Oshawara took the position that if he was to learn English it would only make sense to learn it from an Englishman, even on tape.

He had the phrase book that went with the lessons in his pocket, but it gave him no confidence. Things like, "May I see the wine list?" and "Could you direct me to the police station?" were all very well, but they seemed unlikely to be of much help in the present circumstances.

The fellow probably won't come all the way up here, he thought. Still, if he does, it will be a chance to get in some practice. He tucked away his lunch-wrappers and began to leaf through his phrase book, looking for greetings.

Father Morrissey trudged up the hill deep in thought, shedding sparks. He had just spent an hour with a pair of American oil men, and it had left him puzzled and disturbed. Schultz he knew— a slick public relations man for Mogul Oil, full of smarmy affability. The other one, a big fellow with a burn or scald down one side of his face, was some sort of consultant, and they both had something to do with the development meeting that was coming up. No matter how much Father Morrissey had insisted that he knew nothing about the meeting and— though this was not entirely accurate— that he wanted nothing to do with it, the two had gone on prodding and questioning obscurely. They wanted something— but what?

Then, those information kits were arriving at homes all over the parish and rumours were almost as numerous as the kits. Mogul was going to drill for oil on the Shore. Mogul was going to stop drilling entirely and move away. There would be thousands of jobs. There would be no jobs.

Besides the obvious speculations, there were more concrete stories of lost papers and people going around trying to find them, and other stories of cash prizes, or possibly rewards of some kind.

And several of Father Morrissey's parishioners had told him that they had heard on the radio that one of the oil companies was going to build something right away in Parsons Arm. They had different versions of what it was going to be, but they were unanimous in their outrage that it should be planned for the only Protestant community on the Shore. Something was going on, all right, but for the life of him he could not figure out what it was.

Oshawara realized with some nervousness that the man in black was indeed coming up the path directly toward him. He was wearing one of those plain white collars with no tie, identifying him as a priest of one of the many Christian sects. Oshawara had seen many of them in the movies: strange, intense men given to playing baseball and American football and having unsatisfactory relationships with women. This one, however, did not look much like an athlete or a lover. His eyes were on the ground, and he seemed preoccupied; meditating, or praying, or whatever Christian priests do. Oshawara took a last look at his phrase-book. *Good morning* wasn't right, which was a shame, because he had practised that and felt he had it down pretty well. But it had to be *Good afternoon*, unfortunately, and he dreaded the thought of that ugly little cluster of consonants. He formed the words soundlessly and squared his shoulders.

Father Morrissey looked up and realized for the first time that there was somebody on the top of the hill ahead of him. His mind was still preoccupied, but he smiled automatically. "Lovely day," he said.

Oh God, thought Oshawara, and abandoned *Good afternoon*. I'll just have to try it. Just imagine it's one of the lesson tapes. He took a deep breath. "Rubbery dayu," he said, with a bow and a smile.

They stood for a moment, both smiling, neither very sure what to do next. Father Morrissey took in the fact that the stranger was Oriental, was dressed in clothing that looked as though it had come from the Eddie Bauer catalogue, and was surrounded by what looked like an expensive array of photographic equipment.

"Taking some pictures?" he said redundantly, when nothing more appropriate suggested itself.

Oshawara caught the last word and the gesture toward the camera. He bowed again. "Ah so," he said, having found that the expression seemed to work as well in English as in Japanese. "Ah so. Photo-crap."

There was another pause. That doesn't seem to be quite enough, Oshawara thought. Some polite pleasantry seems to be called for. Well, you can't go far wrong telling people you like their country. He gestured inclusively at the scene below. "Is booty-fu," he said.

"Ah, yes," said Father Morrissey, grateful that the other had broken the silence. "It is beautiful, isn't it?"

"Very booty-fu," Oshawara repeated with conviction. "Very white."

Father Morrissey's brow wrinkled. White? He looked down at the town. The church was white, certainly, and his house, but only a few of the others. Could this be a racial reference? Was this smiling Oriental commenting on the fact that all this beauty and affluence was the property solely of Caucasians? Perhaps he was not Japanese as Father Morrissey had at first thought, but from one of the poorer Asian countries.

In fact, Oshawara's train of thought was running along quite different tracks. To his eyes, the stark cliffs and empty barrens had a primitive and forbidding quality that he had been trying to capture in his photographs. There was none of the harmony of man and nature that characterized rural areas of his own country. The haphazard, raw-looking cluster of wooden houses looked precarious and threatened, and the fact that he had seen practically no living things except sea birds all morning added to a feeling of menace, as though something elemental and untamed was lurking in the patches of dark spruce.

"There are enemas?" he asked.

Father Morrissey was used to somewhat alarming statements popping up suddenly in conversations with his parishioners. This, though, was well beyond the usual bounds of unexpectedness. He kept his expression carefully neutral, but eyed the Japanese photographer warily.

"White enemas," Oshawara added earnestly, by way of explanation.

As part of his work with the Citizen's Coalition Against Pornography Father Morrissey had seen a number of publications described by magazine distributors as "adult material." He had also read court

120

transcripts of the trials of some of his brother priests who had been charged with sexual offenses. He was aware that in some unfortunate men carnal desire could take very strange forms indeed. For a long minute he said nothing, gazing at the stranger with a look of mingled compassion and horror. Meanwhile, a more logical corner of his brain ticked over, reached a conclusion, and passed it forward into consciousness. Comprehension broke through, and with it a feeling of relief expressed in a rush of words.

"Oh," he said. "I see. *Animals.* Yes, of course. *Wild.* Wild animals. Yes. I mean, no. No wild animals. Well, some. I mean, there are moose, certainly. We do see the odd moose. And rabbits. But nothing that you'd call wild animals, no. Well, I think there might be lynx or something...," he trailed off, aware that he had probably not made himself very clear.

Oshawara had been listening attentively, but to no avail. This priest certainly did not sound anything like his English teacher at college, and even less like the voice on his cassettes. Maybe it's some sort of dialect, he thought. I wonder what all that was about? Maybe he's warning me about bears or something. Oshawara looked around a little nervously. Still, he doesn't seem to be worried himself, he thought. Maybe a little agitated...he inclined his head in what he hoped would be a non-committal gesture. "Ah so," he said.

"You're a tourist?" Father Morrissey hazarded, after a moment. It seemed unlikely, but he was anxious to change the subject.

Now, that's better, Oshawara thought. If we could stick to nice short things like that, we'd be all right. "Oh, not," he said. "Not are toulistu. Are engineelu." He gestured toward the water and moved his hand up and down to indicate waves. "On sea." Then, feeling that some further courtesy was required, he introduced himself with another small bow. "Mitsuru Oshawara."

As this last exchange was going on, Father Morrissey absent-mindedly rolled another cigarette and lit it. Oshawara watched, at first with interest and then with alarm as a large piece of burning tobacco lodged on the priest's shirt-front. To bring something like this to the attention of a stranger with due politeness would be difficult even in his own language. One could hardly point it out directly: it would require a good deal of roundabout courtesy.

He inclined his head in Father Morrissey's direction, and after immense concentration said, "Excuse, prease, honoured sir. Fire are in your crothing, I berieve." Even as he said the words, he knew they were not coming out properly. He smiled again, nervously.

The priest, if that is what he was, obviously did not understand. He also inclined his head, imitating Oshawara's gesture. By that time the ember had burned itself out. "I see," said Father Morrissey. "You're from...ah...Japan?"

"Ah so. Jopon," Oshawara said. "Very far," he added, and then wondered if this would sound patronizing, as though the man in the black suit would not know where Japan was. It worried him, but he could think of no way to do anything about it.

Father Morrissey began to add up his impressions. Although Oshawara regarded his photographic equipment as an adequate if somewhat out-dated outfit for a serious amateur, to Father Morrissey's eyes it looked decidedly complicated and professional. Propped open on a rock was a leather-bound notebook in which Oshawara had been entering technical data on his photographs, brief descriptions, and bits of poetry and *haiku* that came to him as he composed his pictures. On one of the open pages was a neat little sketch map of the harbour and town, labelled in Japanese with a technician's precise characters.

The rumours of oil development ran through Father Morrissey's mind. An engineer! "You're making a plan?" he said.

Oshawara was heartened. He was a methodical man, and it pleased him that in spite of obvious difficulties, they were occasionally managing to communicate. This isn't as bad as I thought it would be, he decided. If I could do this sort of thing more often, I'd soon get the hang of it. Those cassette lessons are all very well, but as in everything else, there's nothing like practical experience in the field. He would use this as an illustration for his bookish young Third Engineer who was so reluctant to get his hands dirty.

Now, then. *Plan.* He remembered the word very well. In technical drawings, it's a view from above, and that's just what I'm getting here. Simple.

"Ah so," he agreed. "Pran." His camera was set up for a wide-angle shot of the whole area. Just a record shot, really; he was much more interested in closer, more artistic compositions, but a plan view it certainly was. He gestured widely to the scene below. "All," he said. "Tree. House. Water." He looked around for more things to name, and his eye fell on the sheer rock faces dropping into the bay on the other side of the harbour. "Criff," he added.

Father Morrissey followed this inventory in appalled fascination, his mind's eye seeing bulldozers ripping into the peaceful green turf, and vast, if vaguely-conceived industrial things shouldering the little houses aside.

He tried hard to keep his voice casual. "Sounds like a big development."

Oshawara was delighted. They were getting along famously. He thought of the several rolls of exposed film in his camera case. "Ah so!" He nodded vigorously. "Much deveropamen." He thought also of the cost of chemicals and paper. "Much money," he added, and smiled ruefully.

Yes, Father Morrissey thought bitterly. Much money indeed. No use getting angry at this foreign engineer, though— he's only doing his job, poor fellow.

"What's it going to be?" he asked. "A service centre? Rig-building site?"

Oshawara's smile faded. Things were getting difficult again. That was obviously a question, but he hadn't caught a word of it. He assumed an exaggerated look of puzzlement and concentration. "Excuse, prease?"

Yes, thought Father Morrissey again. He's not going to give anything more away. I'm surprised he's told me as much as he has, but I suppose he had to tell me something, with me catching him up here surveying the whole bloody harbour. That's probably why they sent somebody who doesn't speak much English. He can always claim he doesn't understand. "Oh, nothing," he said, rather coldly. "Nothing at all. I hope you enjoy your stay."

"Oh, yes," said Oshawara eagerly. "Much enjoy, thank you." He noticed with regret that the priest was turning to go. Seems sort of annoyed or something, Oshawara thought. Maybe they don't like people taking pictures. But he didn't seem to mind at first. Too bad he's leaving just as I was getting along so well. "Is very booty-fu," he called after the departing priest. "Good-bye, prease."

Father Morrissey did not turn.

Oh, well, Oshawara thought, a little downcast. Still, that was pretty good. Maybe I should stop in at some little country inn on the way back, if I can recognize one, and try talking to the inn-keeper. He might be easier to talk to than a priest.

Father Morrissey trudged down the path, even more deeply in thought than when he had come up.

Shortly after, Oshawara pushed open the door of Johnny Dinn's SeaVue Lounge, rather proud of himself for having recognized the beer advertisements outside.

He hesitated for a moment just inside the door. The dim, windowless interior had none of the charm he associated with the idea of a country inn. It looked to him rather more like the sort of place where movie cowboys hurled each other onto collapsing pool tables while the bartender crouched behind his bar as bottles exploded and mirrors shattered. Still, when one is in another country.... Rather nervously, he approached the bar and placed his carefully rehearsed order.

A few minutes later he was speeding down the road toward the city, leaving behind a beer that he had barely begun to drink, already composing in his mind the story he would tell his shipmates at dinner about his narrow escape.

XI

The rumour of the missing papers continued to go the rounds of the gossip market but, unlike most such stories, no new information was being added to it. Only Bannister, Jarvis, and Schultz knew the truth—or, in the case of the latter two, something close to the truth—and they, of course, were not talking. Unable to feed on fact, the rumour fed on speculation and spawned a whole folklorist's collection of versions, each a little different from any other. On the whole, this worked to the advantage of Bannister and his unwelcome allies, for the variety and volume of the stories created a general atmosphere of confusion within which they could go about their business; not without difficulty, since the rumour mill focused attention on the Hard Shore, but at least without threat of immediate exposure.

Most of those who played with the rumours were motivated by idle curiosity and the desire for some sort of scandal, but some had more concrete interests. Journalists hoped that the whole thing would solidify into a story that would get them on The National or into the pages of the *Globe and Mail*. Conservationists hoped for revelations that would bring the oil companies to their knees, and opposition politicians for information that would do the same for the government.

Sharing both of these hopes was a handful of people too amorphous to be called a group and, although intensely interested in politics, too far removed from its formal processes to be called politicians. They were mostly young and university educated, with strongly developed social consciences that led them to adopt a range of ideologies outside the main stream, from Marxism to Liberation Theology. Their views were too diverse for them ever to form a party or an organization, but they were held together in a loose network of association by a shared belief that the world could be made less beastly, and by a love of arguing over the means by which this could be accomplished. If they were forced to think of themselves collectively, they tended to use phrases like "People on the Left."

Over coffee at the Duckworth Lunch or jugs of beer at The Ship, they built the rumours into their customary discussions. The idea that a large multinational company might be having some difficulty was pleasant to contemplate.

"Wouldn't it be great," someone said at a late-night party in the kitchen of a dilapidated, partially restored downtown house, "wouldn't it be bloody great if Mogul Oil or one of those outfits really had lost something important? And if we could find it?"

"Go on, girl," said someone else. "Sure, that's only a lot of rumour. I wouldn't be surprised if they started it themselves."

"Rumour or not," a third put in, "there's something going on. You just talk to anybody from The Shore."

"Listen," said the first speaker, "why don't some of us go down there and have a talk with Father Morrissey? He's a progressive sort of a...."

"Go 'way with you," the sceptic interrupted. "Don't be so bloody naive. The Church always was the instrument of the ruling class, and it still is. You don't want to be taken in by guys the like of Morrissey."

"Don't give us that nineteenth-century bullshit. This is the 1980s, buddy! Look at Nicaragua. Look at what the Bishops have been saying about unemployment!"

"Oh, grow up, for God's sake! A few guys in purple dresses give out a few lines about how workers shouldn't get screwed too much or too often, and you start falling all over yourself. What have they got to say about women? And abortion? And...."

Several others were about to join in, but the original speaker was not to be distracted. "Give it up, will you?" she said. "I'm not asking anybody to join a convent. All I said was that Father Morrissey is— well, at least you can talk to him. He was out to the rally last week on military expansion in Labrador." She turned to some of the rest of the group. "What do you say we take a run down The Shore tomorrow? Maybe we can learn something."

Nothing so formal as a decision was taken, but on the following day a small group of People on the Left called on Father Morrissey. He was glad to see them, and they had a nice chat. No new information came to light, but they learned of the upcoming development meeting, and resolved to attend.

The visit was duly reported to Sergeant Johnson of the RCMP, who received it with a heavy sigh.

Sergeant Johnson sighed a lot. He was not a very happy man. The last fifteen years as the sole representative of the RCMP Security Service in Newfoundland had not been easy ones for a dedicated policeman who had started his career with high ambition. He had spent a lot of time reflecting bitterly on the piece of bad luck that had caused him to be exiled there, piddling away his best years on the force, denied access to assignments that would bring promotion, derided by his colleagues when he visited the Mainland as "The Newfy Spook," and putting in his time keeping tabs on a bunch of natural-food nuts with babies strapped to their chests whose most subversive activities were protesting the destruction of some old building or holding boring meetings about Ireland or Central America.

He still felt that his plan of disguising himself as an Indian to infiltrate a Native organization in his home province of Alberta had been basically sound. It was just bad luck that he had happened to get splashed with beer during a bar room argument, causing his make-up to run. But the Force is unforgiving, and makes no allowance for Fate. Johnson was put quietly on the shelf in Newfoundland, where he was unlikely to perpetrate more such embarrassing mistakes. Unfortunately for him, it also meant that he was unable to make up for the first one. Headquarters would not even let him handle defections at Gander. They sent their own people in.

In spite of it all, Sergeant Johnson had not entirely lost heart. What kept him going was the same thing that fuelled the dreams of thousands of others in Newfoundland: offshore oil and gas. When that got going, there was bound to be Security work worthy of the talents he knew he possessed, and he would be in on the ground floor. The long, patient years of banishment would pay off, and Wilmer Johnson would come into his own. He read Robert Ludlum novels, and waited.

In the real world, however, patience and virtue are rarely sound investments. As the long years went by, Sergeant Johnson began to hear disturbing rumours. He tried at first to ignore them but they continued to take on shape and solidity, until they were rumours no longer. Shockingly, unbelievably, the federal government decided to phase out the RCMP Security Service and replace it with a civilian agency! While Johnson watched helplessly from the eastern fringe, the Service within which he had still hoped to make his mark was dismantled. Most of the SS personal of The Force were discreetly absorbed into the new Canadian Security and Intelligence Service, but no re-assignment came for Sergeant Johnson.

The old Service was not completely eliminated, of course; that would be too much for anyone to expect. But it was reduced to a pale, attenuated skeleton of what it once had been, and Johnson was its last, tiny, eastern extremity, alone and bereft on the Rock.

In a way, his life had not changed all that much under the new regime. He still pursued the same tedious round. On the rare occasions when something mildly interesting happened, other people still came in to handle it. Some of them were even the same people: ex-Mounties now working for CSIS. But it certainly made dreams of promotion more difficult to entertain.

The only thing that prevented him from giving up entirely and joining a private guard-dog and strike-breaking outfit was the lingering hope that offshore oil activity would still throw up something that he could get to first— something big that would show how wrongly he had been judged for all these years. When he really let his fantasies run, Johnson saw himself cracking a case so spectacular that he would not merely be personally vindicated, but would also be the means by which the RCMP Security Division would be revitalized and restored to its former powers. An Inspectorship, even the Director's chair, would not be beyond his grasp then.

So he soldiered on, keeping lists of the same old names at anti-apartheid rallies and nuclear disarmament demonstrations, suffering the humiliation of being recognized and even greeted by name by greying People on the Left who had been attending the gatherings as long as he had; doling out money from his meagre budget to informants who, he suspected, took it in turns to supply him with useless information when their Unemployment Insurance ran out, as a sort of undercover make-work project.

The dream grew harder and harder to conjure up, but it was not completely dead. Sergeant Johnson received the account of the Left's visit to St. Cyril's without any enthusiasm, but he made a note in his book to pay his own call on Father Morrissey.

By the time Bannister was able to arrange an appointment with Loyola Merrigan he was almost looking forward to it. The rest of his affairs were in chaos, but if there was one thing he was confident of, it was his ability to deal with bent politicians. It was a relief to be tackling a task he felt he could handle. Getting the driving charges fixed took on a symbolic significance in his mind— it would be the first step in regaining control of things and getting out of the mess he had landed in.

Normally, of course, he would have checked out his information more fully, but there was no time for that. In any case, he did not want to draw attention to his interest in the MHA for The Shore. Besides, he could hardly have better information than he had. Theresa had volunteered it so innocently and ingenuously that it could not be anything but true. He prepared himself for the interview by rehearsing a few thoroughly obscene jokes and drawing a large wad of cash from his expense account.

Merrigan's legal offices were high-ceilinged, dim, book-lined, and musty. The old lawyer had just returned from an appearance in the Supreme Court, and was dressed in baggy striped trousers and an ancient, threadbare gown that had once been black, now faded to brown around the edges. The ends of a limp, greyish neck band hung unevenly down over a stained waistcoat with several buttons missing. Merrigan peered at his visitor dimly from behind tiny, gold-framed spectacles that seemed to have been surgically implanted among mottled cheeks, blue with broken veins, and an enormous purple nose. All around, Bannister had the feeling of having been projected into a highly realistic movie set for a Dickens novel.

The old bugger seems hardly capable of recognizing a tasty young secretary, Bannister thought, let alone making a pass at one. Still, Theresa had been as definite as could be. And some of these old guys can surprise you.

The old man had been interrupted in the act of rummaging among the untidy stacks of papers and books on his ancient desk. After blinking and squinting at Bannister for a moment he continued his search, breaking off only to wave him to a high-backed chair with a torn leather seat. Bannister sat. Merrigan wheezed noisily and rustled papers. Finally coming up with a crumpled grey cloth like a duster, he blew his colourful nose with a resounding honk and pushed the cloth back into the pile of papers. Along with his stertorous breathing, the old lawyer produced a continuous flow of mutters, grunts, and less clearly definable noises within which Bannister thought he detected an invitation to state his business.

"Nice place," he said. He was finding it hard to begin. "Some nice...uh...stuff." He jerked his head suggestively toward the door to the outer office, where three rather ordinary young women had been working when he entered. Merrigan appeared not to have heard, and seemed to be hypnotized by something on the wall above his visitor's head.

Bannister tried again. "Nice to have a bit of young stuff around."

Merrigan emitted a series of grunts that could have been a paroxysm of asthmatic coughing, but might as easily have been a lecherous chuckle. Encouraged, Bannister mentioned that his office, too, was similarly equipped. The old man's wheezing seemed to convey a spark of interest, and Bannister went on to describe Theresa in terms that would have shocked Miss Hiscock to the core. In fact, he was more than a little disgusted himself by what he was saying. A bit of colourful bragging to Al and the boys was one thing, but this cold and calculated recital was something else entirely. Still, if he was going to get through to this apparently senile and possibly deaf old sex maniac, strong measures seemed to be called for.

The interview dragged on. At times Merrigan seemed to be asleep, or even dead, and Bannister found himself leaning forward and perspiring with the strain of trying to reach him. At other times the old man seemed to revive and with much effort and heavy breathing remember where he was, and ask a question.

Several times he took out an ancient fountain pen, elaborately unscrewed the top, and selecting a scrap of paper apparently at random from the yellowing pile in front of him, laboriously wrote something down.

"Hibernian...?" Merrigan croaked.

"Yes. Hibernian International...."

"Inter...nation...al...," the pen scratched slowly along. "Pet...roleum...Ex...pe...dit...ers...." Merrigan looked at what he had written in apparent surprise, as though it were an anonymous and somewhat threatening note that had just been slipped under his door. "Incorporated...?"

"Yes," said Bannister.

Merrigan drew himself up and glared angrily across the desk. "Of course it's incorporated," he snapped. "When, man, when?"

"Oh. This year. I guess."

Merrigan dropped the paper and looked abstractedly at the ceiling. Bannister rather expected him to ask what year it was.

And so it went. Bannister struggled to maintain a jocular, men-of-the-world-together tone. He described his difficulties at Parsons Arm, and the impaired driving charge. He spoke of his company's earnest desire to see that the government stayed in sane and sensible hands, their willingness to contribute to the election expenses of reasonable people, and their complete lack of interest in claiming credit for their support in the form of official receipts. Through it all, he kept up a steady counterpoint of suggestive remarks and sexual allusions.

When he stood up to leave, he pulled a handkerchief from his pocket in such a way that his wad of banknotes slipped out and fell among the jumble on Merrigan's desk. He was afraid for a moment that no one— Merrigan least of all— would ever find it again, but the old lawyer retrieved it with alacrity, examined it with ponderous care, and handed it back to him without a word.

"You have made some interesting suggestions," Merrigan said at last, looking as though he were trying to remember what they were. "Most interesting. You must give me time to consider their...ah...yes, their value...," his voice trailed off and he apparently fell asleep again, this time standing up.

The dirty old bastard, thought Bannister. He wants more! "Yeah," he said, pocketing the bills. "Well, I don't know how much more I can...tell you. Maybe a bit. You think it over, and let me know what you want. Want to know, that is. I guess I'll be hearing from you?"

Merrigan's eyelids lifted slightly, and the dim light glinted off his spectacles. "Oh, yes," he said. "Oh, yes indeed."

Out on the street, Bannister felt a good deal less confident than when he had gone in. Arranging pay-offs was usually easier than this. A cold fog was creeping up from the harbour, and he shivered apprehensively.

For the first time since they had been schoolgirls, Stella Mercer called Miss Hiscock. Ever since either of them could remember, Miss Hiscock had always called her. Over the years, she had built up a view of their relationship in which she saw herself as the only source of comfort and support for her childhood companion.

"She has nobody," Stella would tell people sadly. "No family, and practically no friends. She depends on me." When Miss Hiscock did not call for two nights running, therefore, Stella was unprepared to recognize how much she, herself, depended on their conversations. As she dialled the number, she transformed her feelings into concern for her friend's welfare.

"Oh, there you are," she said when Miss Hiscock answered. "I was wondering if you were all right."

"All right? Of course I'm all right. Why should you...."

134

"Well, when you didn't call last night or the night before, I thought you might be sick or something. I was getting worried about you."

"Oh, good Heavens, no, Stella. I'm not sick. I've never felt better. I was going to call you. It's just that the last couple of nights it was in so late when I got in, and...."

"Late?" said Stella. "Well, you certainly know that I don't go to bed early!" Then, surprised at the note of sharpness in her own voice, she softened her tone. "What on earth have you been up to, Marjorie?"

"Well," said Miss Hiscock, "you know that I've been working with Patri...with Mr. Callahan on this silly business of those missing papers? Yesterday he had a lot of the people in the area bring the envelopes they'd got in the mail to his fish plant— it's really amazing, Stella, how those people will do things when he asks them. They'd do anything for him. He's such a nice man. Anyway, we were checking through all the envelopes, and by the time we'd finished it was nearly seven o'clock, so he suggested that we drive into town for dinner. We came in my car, and he had two young fellows bring his in so he'd have it to go home. We had a lovely dinner at the Stone House. And then, after, we went to the Crowsnest. He's a member there. Do you and George ever go to the Crowsnest, Stella?"

"No," said Stella shortly. She had often wished that George was a member.

"That was my first time. I've heard so much about it. It's a bit strange. Like something out of an old war movie. But it's very nice, really. We met some friends of Patrick's, most interesting people, and the time just seemed to fly by. I was amazed when I got home and saw how late it was."

"Hmph," said Stella. And then, in spite of herself, "What about the night before?"

"It's the funniest thing," said Miss Hiscock. "We went to a play! You know this SUP Hall, or whatever it is they call it— some sort of old union hall or something, down on Victoria Street? I'd heard about it, but I didn't like the sound of it. When Patrick suggested we go there I really didn't want to, but he's been so good about all this business that I didn't like to say no."

"Marjorie!" said Stella, shocked.

"Stella, you wouldn't believe it. They've made the nicest little theatre of it! Of course, it's not the union any more— they've just kept the name. It's some sort of group of actors and artists and things. They've even got a nice little art gallery as a lobby. And the play was really very good. Of course, they put on all sorts of outrageous Bay accents, and the language was a little bit coarse at times. But we did laugh! Patrick goes there quite often, apparently. And then, afterwards, we had a drink at the Newfoundland Hotel, in that place with all the trees and things...."

"Marjorie, you don't think you're seeing too much of this Callahan fellow, do you? After all...."

"Oh, Stella, for Heaven's sake! He's just a very nice man who's being kind. I think he's rather lonely."

The conversation went on until George came home from the Elks Club.

XII

Father Morrissey sipped at his beer. He did not actually care for it— a light white wine was more to his taste, but Johnny Dinn's SeaVue Lounge did not run to anything beyond an occasional bottle of Baby Duck for the Ladies' Darts League. Father Morrissey dropped in at the SeaVue from time to time in the late afternoon or early evening. It was one of many little ways he had of keeping in touch with the life of the parish. Even one bottle of beer sometimes left him with a headache but it was, he felt, worth it to make informal contact with the people on their own terms.

Mostly, though, he did not make as much contact as he would have liked. Nobody seemed to stay in the bar for very long. People tended to have a polite word or two, polish off their drinks, and hurry out on apparently urgent errands. It was good to see such moderation, but a little puzzling, too, because he was well aware that some of his parishioners had problems with alcohol. Quite a number, in fact. He could only conclude that they must do their serious drinking elsewhere. He often wondered how Johnny Dinn managed to stay in business.

Johnny Dinn had his own opinions on the matter, and the money Father Morrissey's visits lost him was deducted from his contributions to Church charities.

Sergeant Johnson entered the SeaVue with more than usually mixed feelings. He was a long way from his childhood in the Red Deer Gospel Hall, but nonetheless the idea of interviewing a clergyman in a bar offended his sense of order. He moved cautiously into the room. He knew Father Morrissey by sight, but there was no need to search for him. There seemed to be nobody else drinking that day—a most unusual state of affairs at Johnny Dinn's.

He bought a beer and carried it over to where a lone figure sat on the far side of the room. "You're Father Morrissey, aren't you?" he said, easing into a chair.

The priest was glad of someone to talk to, even if it was not one of his parishioners. "Why, yes, ah...." He hesitated, feeling that he probably ought to know the man's name. In fact, he had seen Johnson several times at protest meetings and the like, most recently at a demonstration in St. John's against low-level training flights by NATO pilots over Labrador.

"Johnson," said Johnson. "Federal Government. Department of Regional Economic and Social Development." This was his usual cover in rural areas. If people already recognized him, it didn't much matter who he said he was; if they did not, there were enough representatives of various government departments around to make the story credible—even to *bona fide* development workers.

If Father Morrissey had been a dog, his ears and tail would have snapped erect. As it was, he began to roll a cigarette and said, "Development, eh?" and waited.

"Lots of action on The Shore these days, I guess," Johnson said.

"A lot of talk," said Father Morrissey. "The action hasn't started yet," he added darkly, "but it's not going to be long coming."

"I was hearing around the Department," said Johnson casually, brushing a vagrant spark off his knee, "that you had a meeting the other day with... some people from St. John's...."

To Father Morrissey, his visit from the People on the Left had been a pleasant chat with some young acquaintances. The only thing that qualified as a meeting was his encounter with that slick Public Relations fellow from Mogul Oil and his Texan accomplice with the red face. "Yes," he said, trying not to show too much prejudice. "I had."

"What do you think of those people?" Johnson asked.

This was too good a chance to miss. If some federal department of development wanted to know what Gerry Morrissey thought of oil men, industrialists, and all the rest of that unholy crew, he would not be backward about telling them.

"They are," he said, sending a shower of sparks down the front of his cardigan, "the biggest danger to the Newfoundland way of life that we have faced in four hundred years!"

Johnson was completely taken aback. He looked narrowly across the table to confirm that this was indeed the misguided, left-leaning clergyman who hung about the fringes of potentially suspect groups. Was he drunk, perhaps?

"Surely," Johnson said, trying to give himself time to think, "surely that's a bit extreme?"

"Extreme?" said Father Morrissey. "Yes, I suppose you could call the total destruction of Newfoundland society extreme. I would, certainly." His remark had clearly shaken up the government man, and he was enjoying the effect.

Not drunk, thought Johnson. Crazy, maybe. Anybody who thinks that bunch of peaceniks and do-gooders is capable of destroying anything.... But if he thinks like that, why does he hang around with them? I suppose I'd better push it a bit and see how nutty he really is.

"But, really, Father," he said in a placating tone. "There are only a few of them, and...."

"At the moment," Father Morrissey broke in. "At the moment. But they're only the tip of the iceberg. They nibble away with their pamphlets and their meetings and their seminars, and people go along and go along, and forget the kind of organization they've got behind them. One of these days, we'll wake up and they'll have taken over!"

Paranoid, Johnson thought. Definitely paranoid. But Father Morrissey was warming to his favourite subject. "You take that Japanese outfit...," he began.

Johnson choked on his beer. "Do you actually think the Japanese are involved?" he gasped.

Father Morrissey gave a secretive smile. "It's not a matter of thinking. I know. I talked to one of them. Just after I talked to...those others. You seem surprised. I would have thought a man in your position would know all about that sort of thing."

Johnson was shaken. He had been long enough in his trade to recognize absolute sincerity and conviction when he heard it. What the man was saying was insane, but there was no hint of irrationality in the way he said it. The Mountie shook his head in disbelief.

For his part, Father Morrissey was inwardly shaking his head in disgust. Bloody typical, he thought. The government sets up all these agencies that are supposed to be concerned with development, and they don't have a clue what's going on. Obviously, this poor fellow has no idea.

"Look," he said in a kinder tone, "I know the sort of difficulty you people work under. The left hand not knowing what the right hand is doing, and all that. But I'm the parish priest. I hear all kinds of things. I talk to all kinds of people. You'd be surprised at the sort of things I pick up."

In the recesses of Johnson's mind a faint ray of light began to glimmer. There was obviously more to this rumpled, eccentric little man dropping sparks down his shirt than he had ever suspected. Of course! The Vatican has its own intelligence sources. That would explain why he hangs around the lefties. And he keeps talking about how I should know all this, so he must know who I am.

"You say you've actually talked to one of them?" Johnson said.

"I have," said Father Morrissey, rolling another cigarette. He had not enjoyed a conversation so much in years. "And I can tell you, this thing is going to be *big*."

Johnson leaned forward. Could this really be his old dream coming true at last? He found it hard to believe that the woolly-headed, argumentative people he had been observing for so long could be tied into an international terrorist conspiracy to sabotage oil development— but wasn't that just the way these things were supposed to happen? And if Father Morrissey could be an undercover agent for the Vatican, anything was possible. He suppressed a shudder of excitement at the thought of the little priest talking to a cold-eyed, expressionless Oriental with a machine gun under his coat.

"Those Japs," he said, looking furtively around the empty bar, "they're ruthless!"

Father Morrissey drew back. He did not approve of racist language. "They're efficient," he said. "Thorough. They know their job and they do it well. I don't blame them, I blame us. Ourselves, our government— your own organization, if you'll pardon my saying so. That's where the problem lies."

"Yeah," said Johnson. "I can't disagree with you there."

"Well, we just have to do what we can...." Father Morrissey glanced at the clock over the bar. "Oh, good heavens, look at the time! My housekeeper will have my supper on the table. She's like a mother hen about meal times. Nice talking to you, Mr., ah...." He bustled out with a cheery farewell to Johnny Dinn, lurking morosely behind his silent cash-register.

Johnson strolled over to the bar and ordered another beer. "Nice fellow, Father Morrissey," he said.

The bartender grunted noncommittally.

"He was mentioning some Japanese people being around here. Have you seen any?"

"I seen one," said Johnny Dinn. "I don't know was he Japanese or what, but I don't want to see no more like him."

Johnson swallowed with excitement. "Really? Why is that?"

Dinn leaned forward on the bar. "Just the other day, it was. This fella comes walkin' in here, lookin' all around like it was a museum or somethin'. Then he comes over to the bar. 'One grass of beer, prease,' he says. 'What kind?' I says, like you would. 'Yes, prease,' he says. 'One grass of beer.' So I gives him a Dominion.

"Well, sir, Pinky Doyle was over there in the corner, as usual. He'd be here now, only for Father bein' here. So Pinky comes over, large as life. 'Good day to you, sir,' he says. 'And how are you gettin' on? Grand weather altogether for the time of year.' Friendly as bejesus. Pinky's never one to pass up the chance of a stranger buyin' him a drink.

"Buddy looks at him for a minute, sort of sizin' him up. Then he ducks his head, gives a bit of a grin, and says, 'Arsehole.' Just like that. Of course he don't pronounce it quite right, but that's what he says. Cool as you like, no expression on his face, just looks at old Pinky and says, 'Arsehole.'

"Now, I'm not saying there wouldn't be a good many people would agree with him. Pinky Doyle is a fella only a mother could love, and that on a payday. If it was anybody from around here said it, you could understand it. But for a stranger to come out with it like that...." Dinn shook his head disapprovingly.

"So what happened?" said Johnson.

"Well, Pinky stands there for a minute, still grinnin' and friendly. He ain't too quick. But eventually it sinks in. 'Jesus Mary and Joseph!' he says. 'Get down off of that stool and say that!' And he ups with his fists and he's dancin' around throwin' punches at the air like Mohammed Ali. 'By God, we beat yez before in the War, and we'll beat yez again!' he says. Not that Pinky knows anything about the war. Or any kind of fightin' at all, come to that.

"Next thing I knows the stool's gone over sideways and your man is backin' for the door all crouched over, choppin' his hands around and kickin' up his feet like Bruce Lee. Seein' he's backin' away, Pinky takes a lunge forward and gets tangled up in the stool. Down he goes, and the other fella's out the door and gone.

"I don't understand it at all. Man comes in askin' for trouble like that, you'd think he'd stick around when he gets it. Sure, Pinky was no danger to him. Them fellas, you know, they can break bricks with their bare hands. If I ever sees him come in here again, I'm going to call the Mounties."

"I think that would be a very good idea," said Johnson, and made a mental note to ask the local detachment to contact him immediately if it happened.

The date of Bannister's court appearance drew nearer, and still he had heard nothing from Merrigan. Finally, one morning Miss Hiscock informed him that the old lawyer's secretary had called and asked if Bannister could come to see him that afternoon.

Oho, Bannister thought. So he's finally figured out what he wants. Crafty old bugger. I hope it's only money. God, I hope I didn't lay it on too thick about the sex stuff. If he wants me to organize an orgy for him or something....

Since the opening had presented itself, he asked Miss Hiscock if she knew Merrigan. It was an automatic reflex of information gathering.

"Oh, goodness, yes," said Miss Hiscock. "I'm sure everyone knows Mr. Merrigan. He's quite an institution."

"Been around a long time, I guess?" Bannister prompted.

"He certainly has. I've been told—though I don't know whether it's really true—that he was in one of the last governments before the Commission. That would be in 1930 or so. I know he's been in the House since Confederation."

"Yeah," said Bannister. "I hear he's...uh...got a bit of a reputation."

"Well," Miss Hiscock said primly, "he is certainly well known. But when you speak of a 'reputation', it sounds as though you mean something discreditable. That would not apply to Mr. Merrigan."

"It wouldn't?" The routine inquiry was suddenly becoming serious. "I got the idea he might be a little bit...uh...shady, shall we say?"

Miss Hiscock was incredulous. "Shady? Mr. Merrigan? My goodness, who on earth could have told you that?"

"I was talking to Theresa. She's from his district, and she says she knows this girl in his office...."

"Theresa? And she said...?"

"She said he was crooked. 'Crooked as a stick' was how she put it."

"Oh, that girl!" said Miss Hiscock. "Really! After all I've...I'm sorry, Mr. Bannister, but I'm afraid there has been a serious misunderstanding. It's the way these outport people speak. You see, when someone like Theresa says someone is 'crooked', they don't mean that the person is dishonest."

Bannister felt a numb sensation beginning in the back of his neck. "They don't?"

"No. No, they mean that he's bad-tempered. It's the dialect, you know. It's an old-fashioned way of speaking. I blame the schools...."

"So you say she didn't mean...."

"Oh, goodness, no. That's one thing that no one would say of Mr. Merrigan. It's rather surprising, when you think of it, when he's been a lawyer and a politician so long. In fact, people do say that he could have been a lot more successful in both if he hadn't been quite so...so scrupulous. They say that that's why he's never been a cabinet minister or anything. He terrorizes everybody, even in his own party. And his legal colleagues, too, I understand."

"Oh."

"As for being bad-tempered, well, he certainly has a reputation for that. I've heard that even Supreme Court judges are afraid of him."

Bannister nodded dismally. "I'm sure glad you cleared that up. Look, Theresa also said that he's a kind of a...you know, like, a sort of a dirty old man...."

Miss Hiscock was appalled. "Mr. Bannister!" she said.

"Well," said Bannister defensively, "she said he 'gets dirty' with the girls in his office. Said her friend told her."

"Oh, dear! This is really too bad! I must speak to that girl.... It's not her fault, I suppose. I really don't know what they teach them in the schools these days...."

"Okay," said Bannister. "You mean...?"

"I'm afraid she was just adding to what she'd already told you. To 'get dirty' with someone simply means to...to speak sharply to them. To be angry with them, and say unkind things. I'm afraid Mr. Merrigan has quite a reputation for that, too...."

"Oh," said Bannister. "I see."

"Yes. But what a terrible thing for you to have thought! Why, nothing could be farther from the truth. Mr. Merrigan is a very religious man, you know, and he absolutely abhors...that sort of thing. He simply refuses to defend anyone charged with anything involving...indecency. I've heard that the slightest hint of improper language makes him furious."

Bannister reached desperately for the only remaining straw. "Yeah," he said. "I see. But I guess he's pretty senile, by now, huh? Forgetful, and that?"

"Well, he does give that impression. But he's been like that for years. People say that it works very well for him in the courtroom, when he's questioning a witness on the other side. He dodders and dithers, and the witness isn't sure he's paying attention, you see, and often people will blurt out things they didn't mean to say."

"I can see how that might happen," said Bannister, miserably.

"Yes, but at the same time, people say that he has never forgotten a client or a case in his entire career. They say he knows every one of his constituents by name— and their parents and grandparents as well. He's a remarkable man."

"He sure is."

"Oh," said Miss Hiscock. "You've met him, then?"

"I mean, I'm sure he is."

"But, how dreadful that you should have thought such terrible things about him! I'm very glad we've been able to set things right."

"Yeah," said Bannister, feeling the water close over his head. "Me, too."

There was no way to avoid going through with the interview. At Merrigan's office he had to sit quietly and politely while the old man tried to get him to repeat his earlier performance. The set-up was amateurish— Bannister could tell exactly where the microphone was hidden— but he could not help admiring the old lawyer's interview technique. All Bannister could do was blandly avoid all the openings he was given, concentrate on the misunderstandings that had led to the driving charges, and insist— although the words nearly stuck in his throat— that all he wanted was for Merrigan to defend him in court.

Merrigan was obviously disappointed. When it was clear that the oil man was not going to incriminate himself, he grumpily and perfunctorily took the particulars of the case, without writing anything down, and brought the interview to a close.

XIII

_____

Sergeant Johnson was on the direct line to headquarters. Unfortunately, because of the drastic reductions in staff, Inspector Charbonneau was Duty Officer.

"Allo, Johnson," he said. "Still alive out dere, eh? Nobody mistake you for a seal and 'it you on the 'ead?" Inspector Charbonneau laughed immoderately at his own joke. "Hey, Johnson, you know what is the word in French for 'seal'?"

"Yes, Inspector, I know."

"Oh. Funny, eh? Listen, I 'ear a good one the other day. How many Newfie does it take to overt'row the government?"

"Inspector, this is serious." Johnson was almost pleading.

"Oh, you got the wrong number, den. Anyt'ing serious, you call dose other guy—dose CSIS." Charbonneau was also bitter about not having been absorbed by the new agency.

"Please, Inspector, this is really important. I need some help. I need some manpower."

"Manpower?" Charbonneau laughed derisively. "You got the wrong number for sure, Johnson. You know how many people we got left? Altogether?"

"Yeah," said Johnson. "I know. But I'm onto something here that could be big. All I need is a bit of back-up...."

"We all need back-up, eh? Only we don't get it. Dose goddamn politician...."

"If this thing turns out the way I think," Johnson said, "we could leave those CSIS guys with egg all over their faces." He quickly remembered that Inspector Charbonneau either did not or pretended not to understand such English idioms. "Make them look like real dorks," he translated. "I've got something going here, and I don't see any indication that they know anything about it. With a bit of help I...we could bring in something that would make them sit up and take notice."

Charbonneau had no greater opinion of Johnson's powers than any of his superiors, but even a remote possibility of embarrassing their rivals was attractive. "Eggs in their face, eh?" he mused. "What have you got?"

"I can't exactly explain," Johnson began, and hearing Charbonneau draw in his breath to interrupt, he hurried on, "because I haven't got the details myself yet. All I know is that this oil stuff is hotting up again, and I've got some indications that some international baddies may be taking an interest. It could be really big. I've got some tips— strictly unconfirmed, but we've got to follow it up. If we don't, and if it turns out they were right, it's us who would look like dorks." He considered dropping a mention of the Japanese connection, but decided it would be unwise. Charbonneau would undoubtedly be reminded of several Japanese jokes. And in the unlikely event that he took it seriously, he would probably want to take over himself.

"Wait one minute, dere, Johnson! I been reading your reports, you know. How come I don't see nothing about this before?"

"Look," Johnson said desperately, "I've got some new sources of information, all right? It's just breaking.

I need help to check it out. It could be a false alarm, but I don't think so. And I haven't got much time to find out."

"No time? Why not? You got time to write lots of boring report, with nothing in dem...."

Johnson gritted his teeth. "This thing is tied up in some way with a meeting Mogul Oil is having next Wednesday in a little place called St. Cyril's. Something is going on. I'm doing the best I can to keep track of the people I think are involved, but I can't do it all by myself." Some of the People on the Left were inclined to stay up arguing for most of the night, and others to get up at dawn to go jogging, depending on whether they were drinkers or health nuts. Keeping them all under surveillance was exhausting even to think about. "If I could only have a couple of guys, even for a few days...."

Charbonneau grunted and furrowed his brow. Although staff had been cut to the bone, work had been cut even more drastically. He did have a few people around, and they had little to do. Notably, he had two young constables, problem cases who had been recruited just before the creation of the civilian agency, who were not good enough to be absorbed into it and were too short to be taken into the regular force. Without much to occupy them, they had been spending their time getting into trouble. A few days under Johnson in Newfoundland might make them regret having installed optical surveillance equipment in the dressing rooms of the Miss Teen Canada pageant.

"Maybe I can spare a couple of guy," he said. "But this better be good, Johnson. You know what our travel budget looks like dese days?"

"That's great, Inspector. I really appreciate it. Look, there's one other thing. Could you run a check on a priest— a Gerard Morrissey? See if we've got anything on him. Besides my own reports, I mean."

"Dose priest," Charbonneau grumbled. "A few year ago dey was seeing communist under their bed. Now half of dem is communist demself. Hey, did you hear the one about the priest who...."

"I don't like it," Jarvis said. He and Bannister and Schultz were having another of their nightly progress meetings at the HIPE (Canada) offices. "We're going nowhere on this thing. It's been too long. And there's too much attention being put on your Target Area. Everybody and his uncle is poking around. That dumb cop, Johnson, was down there the other day, and if he's taking an interest then there can't be anybody left who doesn't know something's going on. I've been able to keep CSIS out of it so far— they do what we tell them, but if anything breaks they're going to want a piece of it...." He leaped suddenly to his feet and threw open a window. "Do you have to smoke so much, for God's sake? It's impossible to breathe in here!"

Bannister ignored him and lit another cigarette. He was up to two and a half packs a day.

"Yeah," said Schultz. "My people are getting a bit restless too. I keep telling them it's just normal rumour mongering in an area of potential development, but they're not going to buy that for much longer. The whole Shore is buzzing like a beehive. There's more rumours than there are people."

Bannister continued to smoke in silence. Jarvis turned to him. "Well, what have you got to say?"

"What is there to say? The papers are still out there. The situation is no different than it was at the start."

"Oh, yes it is," said Schultz. "Our Community Liaison meeting is next Wednesday, and my people are nervous. They don't like all the rumours. They don't know what's going on, but they're worried. They're talking about sending some of their own people in to look around."

"Oh, that'll be a great help," Bannister sneered. "Maybe we could get the Salvation Army in there, too."

"Time is running out," said Jarvis. "The way I figure it, if you don't turn up those papers in the next couple of days, you never will. Either somebody's thrown them away — in which case Schultz and I are pretty much in the clear, but you, Bronco my friend, have still got a bit of a problem— either that, or somebody's got them, and knows what he's got, and plans to use it. I'd say that by next Wednesday we'll be pretty sure which it is."

"How so?"

"Use your imagination. Suppose somebody's got the papers and is going to make something public. Wouldn't that meeting in the Target Area next week be a good place to do it? Wait until the chairman asks if there are any questions, then bam!" He smacked his fist into his open palm for emphasis. "Lots of witnesses. There's bound to be some press there...."

"Oh, God!" said Schultz. "I'm chairing the question period! And all the Mogul guys will be on the platform! What are we going to do?"

"Bannister keeps the search going, for all the good that's going to be. About the only way he could still get that stuff back quietly is if whoever's got it is deaf, dumb and blind and he trips over them in the street, but we can't afford to overlook any possibility. Then we have the meeting covered like a blanket."

"Covered?" said Schultz in alarm. "How do you mean?"

Jarvis gave him a cold stare. "I mean that if somebody starts to ask a question that sounds like they've got information they shouldn't have, they don't get to finish it."

Schultz went white, his mind filled with images from spy movies— the soft spit of a silenced gun, people milling and screaming, shadowy figures slipping purposefully through the confusion. Jarvis ignored his distress. "I've got a couple of Assistant Pastors coming for a visit. They get here tomorrow...."

Bannister's head snapped up. "Wait a minute, Reverend. I made it clear...."

The preacher turned to Schultz, who was gnawing distractedly on a fingernail. "I don't think there's anything else we need you for. Bronco and I have a few things to talk about."

When Schultz had left, he turned back to Bannister. "Look, my friend, I don't think you've been quite keeping up on the situation here. You've been giving me a pretty hard time the last while. I haven't been liking it, but I've been taking it because you've had me over a barrel. I've had to assume that whatever you've stupidly allowed to go missing involves me and my Agency. And I've had to take the position that it would be best for everybody concerned if you got it back without attracting any attention. It wasn't a great chance, but it was better than the alternatives. However, with every day that goes by it gets less and less likely."

Bannister started to interrupt, but Jarvis waved him to silence. "Right now," he went on, "I'd say the odds are about six to four on the scenario that was scaring Schultz so bad just now, and getting longer every day. It scares me even worse. All he's got to worry about is his job, but my neck is on the line. Now, even you have got to realize that I can't just sit back and wait for it to happen. Right?"

He paused for a moment, but Bannister did not answer. He could see that the preacher had a point.

"Okay," Jarvis said. "So if you want to keep me out of the field, there's only one way to do it."

"What's that?"

"Show me the Master Plan. Prove to me that there's nothing missing that can be traced back to me or the Agency."

Bannister gave a grunt of mirthless laughter. "Don't you just wish I could! Sorry, Rev. No can do."

"Right," said Jarvis heavily. "That's what I thought. And since I don't expect any miracles between now and next Wednesday, I've been doing a bit of worst-case planning. You can't cover that meeting yourself, Bannister, and you know it. Neither can I. We've got to have help."

Bannister slumped despondently in his chair. "Suppose you're right. And suppose your guys are lucky and get hold of the stuff. What good is that going to do? They'll blow the whistle on me, and if that happens I don't give a damn if every secret document in Washington gets blown. I've already told you that if I go down I don't intend to go alone. You'll come with me. And just in case you get fancy notions about arranging any accidents, you should know that I've got a fail-safe set up." In fact, he had made no provision for implicating Jarvis if he were to conveniently disappear, but he knew that the CIA man would expect him to.

"I figured on that," said Jarvis, "and I might as well be frank with you: I haven't quite figured out what your fail-safe is yet. I believe what we've got here is what you'd call a Mexican standoff."

"Something like that."

"All right. But I'm not ready to give up yet. I've had to pull every string in the book, but I think I've got something worked out. These guys I've got coming in, they owe me a few. They aren't going to do anything I don't tell them to do. We've still got a chance."

"So if your guys get the papers," Bannister said slowly, "you turn them over to me? And Houston and Langley don't get to hear about anything?"

"What else can I do? Unless, of course, I can figure how to cut out your fail-safe between now and next Wednesday. That'd be a different ball game." Jarvis grinned unpleasantly.

"I ain't worried about that," said Bannister. "Okay. So we've still got a chance. Let's do it."

Bannister was taking no more active role in the search. He left that to Miss Hiscock and Theresa and spent his days fidgeting in his office, avoiding calls from The' Bishop who wanted to know when Parsons Arm could expect the promised aid on its playground project. Two days before his scheduled court appearance he received a letter from Loyola Merrigan, apparently written on an ancient manual typewriter, with uneven letters and X-ed out errors.

"I have considered the matters you have brought to my attention," it said. "It is my opinion that there are no grounds for defence in this case. I suggest that your best course would be to plead guilty as charged and accept the judgement of the court." The letter was signed in a shaky but florid hand, and accompanied by a bill for $145.83.

At court, Bannister received a stern lecture on the evils of driving while intoxicated, a seven hundred dollar fine, and suspension of driving privileges for six months, all of which was reported with only minor errors in the next day's *Evening Telegram*.

He sat in his office with the newspaper in front of him and his head in his hands. The telephone jangled, but he let it ring. He did not want to talk to Bishop if he could help it— or anyone else, for that matter. The phone stopped, then rang three times, stopped again, and rang twice more.

There was no point in trying to ignore the signal. He engaged his scrambler and started to dial Houston, taking several deep breaths before dialling the last digit.

"Hello, Al. You wanted me? Sorry I haven't checked in lately. Been kind of busy." He held his breath and waited.

"Yeah, I understand, Bronco." Al's voice was strangely gentle and conciliatory. "I know how it is. But I needed to talk to you. We've got a bit of a problem."

Bannister frowned at the receiver in puzzlement. He had never before heard Al refer to any sort of problem in anything less than an outraged bellow. In fact, he had never at any time heard Al speak in the tone he was using. "What kind of problem?" he asked cautiously.

154

"Well, it's kind of hard to explain in a few words. You know that cover outfit you've got up there— that Hibernation International Whatsis— you know that's incorporated in Canada, and it's got these Canadian shares? Forty-nine per cent is held by our cover company here, and fifty-one by somebody up there?"

"If you say so, Al. I don't know anything about all that stuff. I'm just the hired hand, remember? You guys handle all that."

"Right, Bronco. Right. We handle it. But the problem is, you see.... The problem is, the guy who holds the Canadian shares is raising hell. He doesn't know it's a cover. All he knows is that an American consulting company gave him a sweet deal. He figures they just wanted to get past the Newfoundland regulations and get in on the oil play, so they make money and he gets a profit with no hassle."

"Yeah," said Bannister, somewhat relieved. "Well, if this guy is worried that we aren't turning over some work yet, I don't blame him. I should have a half a dozen things going by now, but Mogul won't get off its ass. It's this Schultz guy...."

"It's not that, Bronco. It's you. This shareholder doesn't like you. He wants you out of there."

"What? What the hell is this? I don't even know who this guy is, for Christ's sake!"

"Okay, now just take it easy, old buddy." Al was still speaking gently, as though to a difficult child. "He knows who you are. And other people know who he is— or at least some of them can find out if they want to. It seems he's a respectable businessman up there...."

"So what?"

"Well, the thing is, Bronco, this respectable businessman has been getting leaned on by some old guy in the state— provincial— legislature." Bannister closed his eyes and dabbed at his forehead with a handkerchief. "Apparently this old politician guy is also pretty respectable, and he says you're a moral menace or something. He says you went around to his office, told him a lot of filthy jokes, made obscene remarks about a young girl in your own office— who's the daughter of a constituent of his, by the way— and tried to bribe him to fix a drunk-driving rap for you. That's what he says."

In normal circumstances, Al would by this time have been shouting loud enough to be heard from Texas without a telephone, but his voice stayed unnervingly calm. Bannister could think of nothing to say.

"So, you see, Bronco, everybody's kind of upset, you might say. This old politico is apparently pretty straight-laced and religious and all, and he kind of figures you ought to be deported, or locked up, or hung or something. Apparently he tried to get the goods on you, and couldn't, so he's doing the next best thing. He's leaning on his buddy, the shareholder, who is in turn leaning on our cover outfit here. It's all very messy. We need that cover in Newfoundland, and we don't need this kind of problem."

Bannister still could think of nothing to say.

"A funny thing, now, about all this," Al went on. "This shareholder guy kept calling this politician guy a loyal American. I got a transcript of his calls right here, and that's what it says. Now, just out of curiosity, what the hell does that mean?"

Bannister forced himself to answer. "It's his name," he said in a strained voice. "Loyola Merrigan."

Al said nothing for several seconds. When he spoke, it was in the same mild tone, though his voice was slightly higher. "His name is Loyal American? You sure? Well, anyway, you know him, then?"

"Yeah. He's a...."

"He also says that when you got picked up for drunk driving you'd stolen the bishop's car, only they didn't press charges on that one. There's also something about a parson and his arm, but I can't make head or tail of that. Was there an accident and some preacher got his arm broke or something? Listen, it wasn't that CIA guy, was it? He wasn't in on this, too?"

"Al, this whole thing is a mistake," said Bannister wearily. "The car belonged to a guy they call The' Bishop, only he isn't really. It's his name. And I didn't steal his car."

"Oh. His name. Right. Whose car did you steal, then?"

"I didn't steal anybody's goddamn car. I told you, it was a mistake. He left the keys in it, and...."

"I see. Did he leave the parson in it, too?"

"There's no goddamn parson involved! Parsons Arm is a *place*!"

There were several more seconds of silence. When Al spoke again, he seemed to be maintaining his strangely soft, placating tone only with some difficulty. "I see. A place. Right. Well, how about the sexual harassment of this young girl your office? This politician, whatever his name is, is coming down pretty hard on that, apparently."

"Goddammit, Al, I have never so much as...as looked sideways at that girl!" Bannister's outrage was genuine. This was the one area where he felt completely innocent.

"But isn't she the one you've been telling us about ever since you got there? The one with the big...."

"Aw, come on, Al," Bannister said. "That was just talk. You know. I was just...."

"Bronco," Al broke in, "I want you to know something. I don't know whether you're going to be able to understand what I'm about to say, but I'm going to say it anyway. I blame myself for all this. I remember when you called me when you first got up there, going on about snow and all that stuff. That was a call for help, Bronco, and I didn't respond. I was too caught up in my own petty concerns— too worried about saving face, too busy figuring those CIA guys would make us look silly. I didn't take account that a human being— a *friend*— was calling for help.

"And I'm sorry, Bronco. I want you to know that. This last few weeks I've been doing these seminars. They're run by some people from California. Managerial Sensitization, they call it. It's really opened my eyes. You know how I used to be— always hollering and throwing my weight around? Well, I'm a different person now. You wouldn't believe what these people can do. It's sort of like EST, and meditation, and...hell, I can't explain it, but it's great. They've got a doctor in their outfit, and he's given me some new pills.... Anyways, I'm a lot more...more in touch with myself. I bet you can hear it in my voice."

"Yeah," said Bannister. "I think I can."

"One of the things they have us say over and over is, 'You can't change the past, but you can make a whole new future.' Isn't that a beautiful thought, Bronco?"

"It sure is, Al," said Bannister tonelessly. "It sure is."

"Now, I don't want you to worry about this any more, Bronco. I'll be up there next Wednesday. I'd come sooner, only...."

"You're coming here?"

"It's the least I can do, old buddy. We can square things with this shareholder guy, clear up any misunderstandings with the politico...." Al was apparently struck by a sudden thought and his voice lost some of its syrupy tranquility.

"That's all there is, isn't it, Bronco? Just the politician guy, and the car, and the drunk driving, and the parson, and the girl? There's nothing else I ain't heard about yet?" By the time he finished, his voice was rising to something like its normal tone and volume.

"Oh, yeah, Al," Bannister said. "What else could there be?" He chuckled hollowly. "Everything's fine. Really, all that stuff is just a bit of misunderstanding. I can handle it. There's no need for you...."

"Now, not another word, Bronco. Not another word." Al had reverted to his Managerial Sensitization voice. "I owe this to you. I'm going to straighten it all out, personally. And you can just go on vacation. Get a good rest. These people that have helped me so much, they've got other courses, too. You could take one of them...get in touch with your real self. Get yourself really together. I'm going to pull Harrison out of Saudi, and...."

"I'm telling you, Al, it's not necessary. Everything is under control. I *am* in touch with myself, for Christ's sake!"

"Bronco, Bronco. Don't excite yourself. I can hear the tension in your voice. We're taught to be sensitive to that. I can hear the strain. The loneliness and anxiety. The fear. I can feel the burden you are carrying, and it makes me ashamed because I know it's my fault...partly, anyways. As of right now, I want you to consider yourself on sick leave, with full benefits. Whatever you're doing, forget it. It can wait. Whatever you were going to do, don't do it. You're going to be looked after, and nobody's going to know a thing about it except me. Go to the beach. Relax. All you have to do is meet me at the airport on Wednesday."

Bannister looked at the cold rain lashing across his office window and gathered the last of his strength.

"There's no beach, Al. Look, you don't have to do this. I'm just fine. Anyway, Wednesday's the day Mogul is having that big public meeting in the Target Area...."

"Great. You can take me along— if you're feeling up to it, that is. I'll get clued in so's I can brief Harrison, and by Friday at the latest you'll be on a plane heading south without a care in the world."

"Yeah," said Bannister. "Thanks. A lot."

"Don't thank me, Bronco. All I want is to see you well and happy again. That's all the thanks I need.

"You know," he added almost shyly, "I'm going to tell them about this at the seminar tonight. Oh, no details or names, or anything, of course. But I'd like to share this with them. Show them what a change they've made in my life...."

Bannister reached for a fresh packet of cigarettes.

Even though Miss Hiscock was hardly ever at home in the evenings any more, she made a special effort to call Stella Mercer regularly. "Poor Stella doesn't get out very much," she told Mr. Callahan, "and she really enjoys hearing about things that are going on. She depends on me, in a way."

One evening Miss Hiscock told her friend about some plans that had been finalized that afternoon.

"Marjorie!" Stella interrupted. "Do you actually mean to tell me that you intend to go to Montreal with this Callahan fellow?"

"Oh, for heaven's sake, Stella! You make it sound like an assignation or something! Patrick has to go to arrange financing for the expansion we...he's planning in the fish plant, and he'd like to have somebody with him who knows French, that's all. Mine's a bit rusty, but I've kept it up fairly well. It's the least I can do after he's been so kind over all this other business.

"I've always loved Montreal," she added in the same explanatory tone, as though this were another obvious and compelling reason for the trip. "We'll stay at the Chateau Versailles...."

"One room or two?" said Stella in a rather nastier tone than she had intended.

"Oh, Stella, really! You *can* be childish at times. Anyone would think you were still back at Spencer."

"Hmph," said Stella. "But can you just go off like that? How about your job?"

"Oh, didn't I tell you? I'm going to give my notice. It really hasn't been a very suitable position, you know, Stella. It hasn't turned out at all the way Mr. Bannister described it. And besides...well, the fact is that with the expansion Patrick is planning, he's going to need a whole re-organization of the plant office. Larger staff, computerized accounting, all that sort of thing. The people he has are very good, but he needs somebody with experience at managing a larger office...."

"Marjorie!" Stella was overwhelmed. "I certainly hope you know what you are doing!"

"Oh, I think so," said Miss Hiscock, with maddening complacency.

George had already come home and gone to bed, but Stella was not ready to abandon the telephone yet. "Well, I don't know, I'm sure. I do hope.... Anyway, I suppose it will be a relief for you to get away from that dreadful little girl Theresa."

"As a matter of fact," said Miss Hiscock, "Patrick and I have been discussing that. I really don't feel right about leaving her alone in that office with Mr. Bannister. I've been hearing the most disturbing things about him lately. Do you know, he was actually convicted of impaired driving? And if half of what Mr. Merrigan has been saying about him is true...."

She went on to outline what Mr. Merrigan had been saying. Stella listened avidly, interjecting with "Dear me!" and "Really?" to prolong the account.

"Yes," said Miss Hiscock. "So, you see, it really wouldn't be suitable for her to stay there. Patrick knows Theresa's family quite well, and thinks very highly of them. He's very concerned."

"Yes, but surely he can't do anything?"

"Well, with the expansion there will be some new jobs in the plant office.... Now, I know what you're going to say, Stella. I have said some rather harsh things about Theresa. But, you know, it hasn't really been all her fault. She's basically quite intelligent, and she's shown a great deal of initiative in this silly business of those missing papers. I think that in the right setting she could do very well."

"Marjorie," said Stella, "I really don't understand you any more. You've changed."

"Yes," said Miss Hiscock. "I think I have. And I think change is a very good thing. You know, Stella, you really should get out more...."

XIV

The meeting on The Shore was extremely well attended. Most unusually, the hall began to fill well before the advertised hour of seven-thirty, and by the time the main body of locals began to arrive at about a quarter to eight, most of the seats were already taken.

Several media people from St. John's were there, including a CBC camera crew. Pastor Jarvis came with two alert-looking men of indeterminate age in white shirts and ties. Patrick Callahan attended, of course, as a prominent citizen of the area, and it seemed natural that, given her interest in the subject, Miss Hiscock should be with him. The' Bishop and John and a contingent from Parsons Arm filled a whole row of chairs and exchanged guarded neighbourly greetings with representatives of the Development Association, who bustled about arranging seats and setting up the stage. Another row was taken up by People on the Left, most of whom nodded, smiled, and waved across the room at Sergeant Johnson, who flushed and tried to ignore them and hoped that his two temporary assistants, seated separately in other parts of the hall, would not notice.

Bannister had been forced to admit that his licence had been suspended, so Al drove them to the meeting, talking all the way about the marvels of Management Sensitivity and the need for Bannister to get in touch with his feelings.

Loyola Merrigan was there, untidy, abstracted, and myopic as ever, but somehow able to recognize every voter and reporter within a radius of a hundred yards, shake their hands, and call them accurately by name. He ignored Bannister, but several times Bannister thought he noticed people the old man was talking to look over their shoulders in his direction with expressions of shock and hostility.

In other circumstances, Schultz would have been delighted by the turn-out. His Mogul Oil colleagues were impressed. They complimented him on a triumph of Community Liaison, but he seemed pale and nervous, and several times suggested to Pete Kelly that the hall was getting too full for safety, and that perhaps the whole thing should be postponed until a larger building could be found.

Theresa and her friends came and found seats on a table at the back. It was not the sort of affair they would normally attend, and they were not sure why they had come, but they were somehow aware that the magical little interlude they had been enjoying, being paid for driving around The Shore talking to people— which was what Jackie, Carm, and Phonse would have been doing anyway— was coming to an end. The meeting seemed to mark a culmination of some sort.

Later, in spite of what happened afterwards, they were heartily glad they had been there. Otherwise, they might have missed the biggest event in their short memories of life on The Shore. When they told the story, they always mentioned that they had several times come close to leaving early and missing all the fun.

The proceedings were, on the whole, pretty boring. It was only the bits of unscheduled entertainment that kept them dangling their feet, nudging one another and giggling at the back: the sound system that, in spite of being tapped and tested a dozen times, exploded in squeals as soon as the first speaker approached the microphone with serious intent; the projection screen that would not stay unrolled for the slide show, and had to be held down by a member of the Development Association squatting uncomfortably on the stage; the

Mogul Oil speaker who had apparently eaten too hasty a dinner, and delivered his prepared speech in the strangled, high-pitched tone of a man suppressing a belch; the periodic thunderous and frequently profane comments that Uncle Bob Crocker addressed to his neighbours in what he thought was a confidential whisper.

When the question period came, Schultz fumbled nervously with the microphone, knocked over a jug of water on the lectern, and flinched every time someone in the audience stood up to speak. The' Bishop took up nearly fifteen minutes with a series of rambling questions about a playground, to which no one was able to supply any answers. Schultz seemed inclined to let him go on indefinitely, but was forced to move to other questioners by a growing chorus of objection from the audience.

The real fun did not begin until the very end. As Schultz was beginning to bring the question period to an early close, ignoring several raised hands, there was a sudden agitation among the cluster of men standing near the door preparing for a quick exit in the direction of the SeaVue Lounge. The little crowd parted, and Father Morrissey pushed through into the hall.

He had not intended to be there, and had said so emphatically for several days to anyone who mentioned the meeting, and to many who did not. Immediately after supper, of which he ate only a few token mouthfuls, he had closeted himself in his study, fully determined to straighten out the parish accounts once and for all, a job that would take the whole evening, and then some.

He had stolen only one brief glance through the window at the scores of cars overflowing the parking lot and parked haphazardly around the hall, and was grimly adding up a column of figures, trying to suppress a guilty feeling of pleasure at the spectacle of Constables Wasylenchuk and Cameron systematically slipping tickets under windshield-wipers, when Mrs. Fagan knocked discreetly on the door and opened it.

He threw down his pencil in disgust. "I thought I made it clear...."

"I know, Father, I know, and I'm sorry to disturb you, I am so. Only...."

"Well?"

"Only, it's old Maggie come to see you, Father, poor old soul. She don't understand about people bein' busy, the poor old creature. And at her time of life, sure you don't know if any time you sees her it'll be the last. I couldn't tell her...."

Father Morrissey closed his eyes and sighed in exasperation. "All right, Mary. Don't go on about it. I'll see her. Send her in."

If the good Lord wanted to try his patience, Father Morrissey reflected, he could hardly have picked a better time or a better instrument. Maggie O'Driscoll was something of a local institution, eccentric, ancient— even older than Brendan O'Leary, and much less photogenic— garrulous and almost impossible to dislodge once she had settled in and begun to talk. With great effort, he produced a smile.

"Well, well, Maggie. It's nice to see you. How have you been?"

The old woman sank into a chair in an untidy heap. "Oh, I hangs together," she said, "with the help of me clothes. Only for me bowels. Sweet Virgin, but I'm pure crucified with 'em."

She went on to expand on this theme in vivid and horrifying detail. When she stopped to draw breath, Father Morrissey quickly interrupted. "I see. Dear me. Have you seen the doctor?"

Maggie shot him a suspicious, bird-like glance. "I thought you *was* the doctor, sure!"

"No, Maggie. I'm the priest." He gave an uncomfortable chuckle.

"Sacred Heart of Jesus!" the old woman exclaimed. "The priest! What'll you think of me at all, goin' on like that about me insides!" She glared at him accusingly.

"I'm ashamed for me life, so I am. Why didn't you stop me, for the love and honour of God?"

When he had first come to The Shore, Father Morrissey had tried to talk to Maggie about her constant invocation of the names and body parts of holy personages, but to no avail. He tried to convince himself that in a person of her age they might be construed as prayer rather than profanity, and left the final decision to a Higher Authority. He smiled wanly and said nothing.

"The priest," she said again in the same accusing tone, as though he had been guilty of some indecency. "And how's a body to know, and you sittin' there in your shirt-sleeves with no collar or nothin'?" She squinted at him narrowly. "You're not Father Malone."

"No." He struggled to maintain his smile. "I'm not. I'm Father Morrissey. Father Malone has been dead for ten years."

"God be good to him," the old woman said fervently. "Sacred Heart, there was a priest for you! You couldn't put nothing over on him!"

Father Morrissey was not in any mood to be told yet again of the virtues of his predecessor. "Yes," he said. "A fine man, I'm sure. So you were wanting to see the doctor. Would you like me to call...?" He reached for the telephone, but he was not to escape so easily. Maggie waved her hand dismissively.

"No, no. 'Tis you I wanted, Father. Only seein' you there with no priest's clothes on, and you after askin' me how I was, I forgot what I was at for a minute. I knows who you are now, right enough." Her tone suggested that he was not what she could have hoped, but would have to do.

She glanced almost furtively around the room for a moment, then burst out: "They're after writin' me a letter!"

"Oh, I see," said Father Morrissey in a kinder tone than he had managed so far. "Well, I know the trouble you have with your eyes...." In fact, Maggie's eyes were sharper than most, but on the rare occasions when she received anything written other than her pension cheque, they seemed to give her trouble. It was one of the small fictions by which she maintained some scraps of dignity in a world where reading and writing were taken for granted and the more solid accomplishments acquired in a lifetime of toil were not much valued.

"I'd be happy to look it over for you." He held out his hand.

Maggie did not produce the letter immediately. She clutched her battered shopping bag closer. "A jeezly great long letter. Pages and pages of it. You'd be half the day readin' it." Her lip trembled. "Nobody'd write a letter like that, only if it was serious." She looked desperately around the room, as though in the hope that Father Malone might miraculously appear to set things right. "I'll tell you, Father, if they're takin' away me pension, they might as well kill me outright and be done!"

Maggie had begun receiving the old-age pension before most of the residents of The Shore had been born. The cheques had begun to arrive, as far as she was concerned, out of the blue. Never before had she received anything that she had not earned with sweat and suffering, and for nearly thirty years she had lived with the conviction that it was all a mistake— that one day someone, somewhere, would discover what was going on and put a stop to it. Mistake or not, however, she was not going to give it up without a struggle.

"Oh, come now, Maggie," said Father Morrissey. "I've told you a dozen times. They can't take away your pension. You're entitled to it. It's probably just one of their long-winded forms again...."

"You don't know the half of it, Father. They sent it to me— oh, a week or two ago. So I takes it home, and I looks at it, and I puts it under me bed, thinkin' maybe they'll forget about it. But they didn't." A tear spilled over and disappeared into the maze of wrinkles on her cheek. "They started comin' to me house askin' about it. And people on the street talkin' about it. And everybody after sayin', 'Mag, did you get a letter?' I told 'em I never seen it. That's a sin, I suppose. Lyin'." She looked at the priest half in supplication and half in defiance.

"Not such a great sin, Mag, in the circumstances," said Father Morrissey gently. "You mustn't get yourself agitated. There's been all sorts of people going around asking about letters, lately. Everybody...." He stopped in mid-sentence, his mouth still open. All the talk and rumours of missing papers! He swallowed several times before he was able to go on.

He came around the desk, sat down beside the old woman, passed her a kleenex and patted her hand. "Now, you just let me have a look at this letter. I'll get Mrs. Fagan to get you a nice cup of tea, and I promise you, we'll straighten it all out." His heart gave a bound as the old woman reached reluctantly into her bag and drew out a thick brown envelope with the logo of Mogul Oil.

Twenty minutes later Father Morrissey was hurtling out the door, clerical collar on crooked and the light of battle in his eye.

"I thought you wasn't going to that old meeting," Mrs. Fagan called after him, aggrieved at being left alone with Maggie, who was now, her spirits fully restored, firmly installed in a chair in the kitchen, cheerfully absorbing tea and reporting in full— as woman to woman— on the state of her intestines.

"Changed my mind!" Father Morrissey called back over his shoulder.

Much as Schultz wanted to bring the question period to an end, he could not ignore the parish priest. Father Morrissey had barely begun on a question that promised to be as long and rambling as any of The' Bishop's, when there was a soft thumping sound, the floor heaved like the deck of a ship hit by a sudden wave, and the front of the hall began to fill with smoke.

Women screamed, men shouted orders to no one in particular, chairs were overturned. Schultz threw himself flat on the floor with his hands over the back of his neck. Father Morrissey had to be led out of the building, still trying vainly to ask his question. Outside, all was confusion. Practically all of the volunteer fire department were at the meeting, and they found themselves incongruously running away from the scene of the fire, up the hill to get their equipment. There were shouts, curses, and the blaring of horns as cars parked close to the hall were moved, and then moved again to get out of the way of the fire truck when it finally arrived with the returning firemen.

By that time the wooden building was well ablaze, and the fire fighters could do no more than hose down nearby houses and cars that had not been moved in time, to keep the flames from spreading.

Father Morrissey helped to comfort some older people who had been shaken by all the excitement, and by the time he had ascertained that none of them were in immediate need of his professional services and that nobody had suffered any real injury, the media people had got their pictures and eye-witness reports and were rushing off to meet deadlines.

He tried unsuccessfully to tell several bystanders about his discovery, but since he had not brought the papers with him and had only scanned their contents, he was not able to make much of an impression. Attention was still focused on the fire, and no one was interested in stopping to chat with the priest— especially since what he was saying sounded pretty much like what he always had to say about oil companies and development. He did not notice that every time he spoke to someone in the crowd, a trim, neatly dressed stranger was at his elbow.

After being asked for the third time, courteously but firmly, to "Just stand away, there, Father, while we gets this hose through," he stood for a moment on the edge of a large puddle of mucky water spreading out from the burning building, frustratedly scanning the faces of the spectators for someone who would listen. The next thing he knew he was lying almost full length in the mud.

He allowed himself to be picked up and fussed over, speechless with incredulity. Someone had absolutely and unquestionably pushed him! He glared malevolently around. Several pre-adolescent boys were skylarking in and out among the crowd, none close enough to accuse. Father Morrissey gritted his teeth. His dignity was already damaged enough. He would say nothing, but there would be some rough sessions coming up in the boys' Grade Five and Six religious instruction classes. Brushing aside his concerned helpers and ignoring the poorly-disguised grins on the faces of several bystanders, he stalked off up the hill, determined to familiarize himself with the document that had fallen into his hands and call a press conference in the morning.

At the edge of the crowd watching the fire, Bannister felt himself nudged by a large, shadowy figure with teeth that gleamed in the firelight. "Looks like I called it pretty close," Pastor Jarvis said softly, "but I didn't expect it to be Morrissey. Of course, you and Schultz were keeping tabs on him. I should have known you'd mess it up. Anyway, it shouldn't be hard to get the stuff away from him."

"Yeah," Bannister whispered. "He seems to be headed home now. I'll...."

"Forget it, Bronco," Jarvis said. "My boys will handle it. It's a job for professionals," he added nastily.

"Well...okay. But look, I need to have that paper fast!"

"Yes, I can see that. That's Big Al from Houston isn't it? Over there giving the Fire Chief advice on how to manage his department? I can see why you might be in a bit of a hurry."

"Yeah. Now how soon...?"

"Not so fast, my friend, not so fast. Things have changed a bit since we talked last. You've been threatening to blow the whistle on me if your boss got to hear about your little difficulty, but I wonder if you still could? You've lost a lot of credibility lately, my friend. Drunk driving, possible car theft, moral turpitude, attempted political corruption.... You are not exactly a highly reputable source any more, are you?"

They had been talking in whispers, both facing the fire, but now Bannister jerked around involuntarily to face the preacher. "I could still make life pretty rough for you, Jarvis. And don't forget my fail-safe...."

"Oh, I haven't forgotten it. Not at all. Been thinking about it a lot. One thing that really puzzled me was why you seemed so confident I wouldn't be able to figure out what your arrangements were, but now I think I've got the answer."

"Yeah?"

"Yep. Seems to me the only way you could be that confident is if there weren't any arrangements to figure out."

"That's ridiculous!" Bannister's voice was much louder than he had intended, and a few curious heads in the crowd turned in their direction.

"Yes," Jarvis whispered, looking away. "But consistent. You've been in a tight spot, and it would have been tough for you to arrange anything, let alone something I couldn't discover with a bit of work. Right now, my friend, I would lay odds of— oh, say about eight to two?— that I've got things figured just about right. I don't think we're in a standoff position here any more at all." The preacher's large hand patted Bannister comfortingly on the shoulder. "Anyhow, let's wait until morning. Then, when I've got the paper in my hand, maybe we can have a little talk. You might have to start being nicer to me. A lot nicer."

Jarvis faded away into the darkness.

XV

A s the flames died down, the crowd thinned. There were little bursts of bad language as the tickets left by Constables Wayslenchuk and Cameron were found, and a last round of parental threats aimed at a few remaining small boys who had been prevented from destroying themselves by going too close when the conflagration was at its height and were now hoping to make up for it by climbing among the steaming ruins.

Locals strolled home or to the SeaVue; carloads of visitors snaked up the hill toward the highway, past the stop sign where Constables Wayslenchuk and Cameron lay in wait. The firemen rolled up their hoses, deploring the fact that the hall's old furnace had not been replaced long since and speculating on whether the blaze would convince the government of the need for a new fire truck.

Theresa and her friends watched until the excitement had died down. The fire had added to the end-of-term feeling that had brought them to the meeting in the first place, and they tumbled back to Jackie's Chevrolet, teasing and pushing. Until now, as they had done their rounds, the two boys had always occupied the front seat with Jackie behind the wheel and the girls in the back. Tonight, however, under cover of an impromptu race for the car, Jackie adroitly maneuvered Phonse into the driver's seat with Theresa beside him, and himself and Carm into the rear. Phonse knew what was intended, and broke out in a cold sweat.

On Jackie's orders, he wheeled the old car up the hill behind the town and into an unused gravel pit, where he backed it into an obscure corner screened by the overhanging branches of a few scrubby trees, and turned off lights and engine. The car was almost completely hidden. Only someone familiar with the place would suspect its presence, but the occupants could observe the whole of the gravel pit through the branches. Before the engine had stopped its usual chuffing and snorting after the key was turned off, Jackie produced four bottles of beer, expertly snapped off the caps, and passed them around. After a moment, there was a creak of springs as he and Carm rearranged their positions.

As the People on the Left fitted themselves into two Ladas liberally plastered with protesting bumper stickers, conversation was desultory.

"Bloody typical. Just the usual load of crap from Mogul. What did we come for, anyway?"

"Oh, well, look on the bright side. You don't get to see a fire like that every day."

"Father Morrissey seemed to be working up to something there, just before the furnace blew up. You don't suppose...."

"You know, come to think of it, just before he fell in the mud he came up to me and Jennie, all agitated— seemed to want to say something, but then some guy came up and told him an old lady was having a stroke or something and he went off. I wonder...."

"What? You think Morrissey's got the legendary missing papers? Don't make me laugh. He was just getting on with his usual politically naive, uninformed, wimpy liberal whining about big development."

"Yeah, I think that whole thing about the papers was a put-on. I wouldn't be surprised if Mogul spread that rumour themselves to get a crowd out to the meeting."

"Well, if they did, it worked. It got us out. Hey, I'm thirsty. Let's stop in for a beer before we head back to town."

"Okay, but listen...."

In the front seat of the Chevrolet, Phonse was in a state bordering on serious panic. The last week or so had been for him a magical time. He had never been popular with girls, being undistinguished in appearance, and having the added disadvantage of being rather shy and slow of speech in a society where quick repartee was the norm. He was not able to keep pace in the endless flow of chatter by which his contemporaries impressed their personalities on one another, and when he did try to contribute he usually stumbled or somehow missed the timing.

He lived in the shadow of the irrepressible and debonair Jackie, whom he admired without reserve. They went everywhere together, but his dashing cousin's success with the opposite sex was the one area of life that he could not share, except sometimes vicariously when he drove Jackie's car down back roads or sat outside it on a rock, smoking cigarettes and looking at the stars while Jackie bid strenuous goodnights in the back seat to Carm or some other girl.

The search for the lost papers had brought Phonse an entirely new experience— spending long periods in the close company of two young women in an atmosphere of comradeship and shared purpose, with the added excitement of a treasure hunt thrown in— and he had found it altogether delightful.

Travelling The Shore in the confines of the old car, the four of them had developed an easy familiarity in which he had been treated almost as an equal. At first, Theresa had been distantly polite and Carm, as Jackie's on-again-off- again girlfriend, had treated him with the contemptuous tolerance of an older sister, but

174

after a day or so things had changed. He knew as much about the households on The Shore and was related to as many people as any of the others, and his opinions on how best to approach this or that difficult case were accepted on a par with everyone else's. Sitting sideways on the front seat with an arm hooked casually over the backrest, he came to be included in the discussion of television programmes and rock groups, and was able to put in the odd contribution of his own without rebuff. He revelled in the delicious sense of intimacy that came of sharing snacks and jokes and gossip.

Central to it all, of course, was Theresa. He watched for her arrival each morning, his heart in his throat for fear she would not appear. He gazed in wonder at the seemingly inexhaustible succession of outfits in which she arrived, each in his eyes more beautiful than the last. He refrained from smoking in the car so that he could breathe the exotic scent of her perfume.

Since Carm and Jackie were a pair, it was almost as though— and he hardly dared to frame the thought— almost as though he and Theresa were, too! Indeed, some of the younger and less sophisticated residents of The Shore had interpreted their daily association this way and commented upon it, sneeringly and yet in a way that conveyed their envy and respect. Phonse sneered back at them, but his heart soared.

Each day, when he thought himself unobserved, he followed Theresa with his eyes, like a savage in the presence of a queen. Every shade of her rather excessive eye make-up and every curve of her bosom were burned on his memory. Each night he lay awake and thought about her in terms that alternated between the impossibly romantic and the almost equally impossible erotic until he fell asleep, when his dreams were like his thoughts, only with the erotic predominating.

Phonse knew that Jackie had deliberately maneuvered him into the seat beside Theresa. He was grateful, but paralysed with fear. He could think of nothing— absolutely nothing— to say. He knew in vivid and living detail what he would like to do, but had not the least idea of how to go about it, nor the least expectation that it would be allowed. To cover his confusion he crouched under the steering wheel to fiddle with the tape deck mounted under the dash, muttering something through dry lips about "having some music" and flicking the buttons savagely to make it appear as though the machine were not working properly—as it frequently was not—to delay the moment when...when.... He felt light-headed, as though he might faint.

Bannister knew that somehow he had to get to Father Morrissey before Jarvis's men. It was his last chance. He lingered at the scene of the fire for as long as he dared, then had Al drive around the little community while he pointed out its sparse points of interest, racking his brain for some plausible excuse for getting away on his own. With remarkable patience, Al squinted out the car windows at the fish plant, church and graveyard, barely visible in the gathering dark.

"Listen, Bronco," he said finally, "it's still early by Houston time. Why don't we go back to your office, and you can clue me in on your files? That'll speed things up. You'll be able to be on the plane that much earlier."

"No!" said Bannister. "I mean, not yet. There's a couple of people I have to see. We better drop in at the bar, here, for a few minutes."

Al gave him an apprehensive sidelong glance, but when he spoke his voice was jocular and humouring. "You don't need to worry about anything like that, Bronco. You're off the hook. Forget about seeing people. Anyways, I don't think it's such a good idea for you to be drinking...."

"Goddamn it, Al, I can't just walk away without saying anything to some of my key contacts, can I? What kind of field procedure would that be? These people will be expecting me. And I told you, that drinking business was all a mistake. But if it'll make you happier I'll have ginger ale. Just pull in over there."

Theresa was annoyed. Not at poor Phonse— she was aware of his suffering, and rather more sympathetic than anything else. In fact, she had come to quite like him. There was more to him than met the eye at first. At times he made himself ridiculous by trying to imitate Jackie's loutish charm, but underneath he was a gentle and rather likeable soul with much more depth than his cousin. And if he could be tidied up a little he could be quite presentable. She found his silent, urgent devotion a pleasant change from most of the boys she met. At least he didn't try to clamber all over her whenever the opportunity presented itself.

At the same time, however, she was not prepared to let him start now, and she was thoroughly angry at Jackie for having put them in this awkward position. She sat rigidly in the passenger seat in a straight-backed posture unconsciously modelled on Miss Hiscock's, frowning at the windshield and trying to decide how best to tear a strip off Jackie without hurting Phonse's feelings. With Jackie and Carm now sunk out of sight in the back seat and Phonse still crouched painfully under the wheel, she was the only one observing the gravel pit.

Just as Phonse was deciding that if he didn't straighten up soon he really would faint, and wondering if he could find some other diversion, such as having an epileptic seizure or falling backwards out the car door and injuring himself, Theresa broke the silence.

"Jeez," she said. "That's some strange."

"What?" said Phonse, raising his head gratefully.

"A car just come in with the lights off, and two fellas got out and hiked off up over the bank and into the bush."

"What? Where?"

"Over there. You can see the car, look. They went up behind, there."

Carm's head appeared over the back of the seat. "Who were they?"

"I don't know. They're not from around here. I think I might of seen them at the meeting tonight, though. Two guys that looked sort of like them Mormon missionaries from the States that comes around."

"I wonder what they're at?" said Jackie. "If they wanted to have a pee, they could do that by the car, right?"

"Maybe they got better manners than some people," Theresa said haughtily.

"Hey, maybe they're, like, gay," said Phonse, trying to match Jackie's suggestive tone. "Goin' off to...do whatever they does...in the woods."

"That don't make no sense," said Jackie. "Why couldn't they do it in the car, like anybody else?" He made a playful grab at Carm, who pushed him away impatiently. "Hey, maybe they're whatsinames— voyageurs. You know, guys who look in windows. Maybe they seen Betty McBride at the meeting and wants to get a closer look at her when she's going to bed."

"Some hopes they got," said Phonse. Then, fearing this might be misinterpreted. "By the time they gets through them woods, they'll be lucky to see her getting up in the morning."

"Yes, I daresay you two knows all about that," Carm said. "Somebody ought to turn you two in to the police."

"Oh, I got better things to do than look in windows," said Jackie with a leer, making another lunge at her.

Carm pushed him away again, harder. "I don't see why everybody's always goin' on about old Betty McBride. She hasn't got nothing the rest of us ain't got."

"No," said Jackie, "only she's got more of it."

"I wants to go home," said Carm.

"Ah, come on, girl. It's only a bit of fun. You knows we loves you."

"Yes, we all knows what you loves, Jackie O'Byrne."

"Well," said Phonse, still anxious not to be considered a voyageur, "I don't know about lookin' in windows, but I do know them fellas is going to have a tough time if they plans to go very far. Jackie and me have set snares in there dozens of times. There's places in there a rabbit couldn't get through."

"They ain't comin' back, though, are they?" Jackie said. "I wonder what they got in that car? Maybe they got a tape deck that works better than this one."

"Now, Jackie," said Carm ominously. "Don't you dare...."

"Ah, take it easy, Carm," Jackie eased open his door. "Just bring the Hard Shore credit card, there, Phonse, will you?"

The two boys slipped out of the car, and Phonse opened the trunk and produced a plastic gas container and siphon hose. He was torn between gratitude for any diversion that would get him out of the seat beside Theresa and the knowledge that she was certain to disapprove of what he was doing.

Theresa, for her part, was fuming. Jackie's behaviour was a clear signal that her period of ascendancy, as the source of paid employment, was over. She had known him long enough to be certain that nothing she could do or say would make any difference. She rolled down her window. "Phonse, I'm ashamed of you! You get right back in the car and take us back to Carm's place, or...."

"Yes," said Carm in fierce whisper. "Both of you get right back in here, or me and Treece are leaving!"

Phonse wavered miserably, the gas container dangling from his hand. Jackie gave a shrug and his most devil-may-care grin. "Do it quiet, then," he said airily.

The two girls got out of the car, pushed through the overhanging branches, and stalked angrily toward the road. "I hopes you gets caught!" Carm spoke loudly over her shoulder, stumbling on her high heels. "I hopes they sends you to jail!"

Phonse looked after Theresa, agonized. Jackie slapped him on the shoulder. "They'll get over it, Phonse, boy. Sure, you can't start lettin' them tell you what to do. You'd have no life at all. Now, we'll just wait a bit. If them two fellas don't come back after all that row, then we'll have a look. Where'd I put my beer?"

In the woods, Pastor Jarvis's two assistants could hear nothing but the sound of their own passage through the dense, tangled growth. They were making much slower progress than they had expected. Their conversation was sporadic.

"Brewster?"

"Yeah, Barker?"

"You a Catholic?"

"No. Congregationalist, I guess. Why?"

"Oh, I just wondered. I figured a Catholic might feel kind of funny, going to break into a priest's house."

"Yeah. I guess so."

"I ain't exactly delighted myself. I hope we don't have to...."

"Don't worry, Barker. It's a piece of cake. The way we're going, he'll be snoring by the time we get there. A touch of the old sleepy gas'll make sure he stays that way, and we're home free. What'll you bet I can lay my hand on that paper within sixty seconds, once we see the lay-out?"

"Ten bucks."

"Easy money. How about twenty if I tell you where it is before we get there?"

"Where?"

"In a big dictionary. Or, failing that, a Bible. Is it a bet?"

"Amazing. You must have taken a correspondence course. Never mind, I'll take the bet. And twenty for me if it's in an inside pocket in an old suitcase."

"You're on. Ouch! Goddamn roots."

Sergeant Johnson drove toward the city in grim silence. He and his two temporary assistants had been watching the most likely People on the Left almost around the clock for several days now. They had watched everything at the meeting, and afterwards had watched the crowd at the fire until everyone had gone. He had tried several times to get close to Father Morrissey during the fire, but the little priest had given no sign that he recognized him. Protecting his cover, Johnson told himself, but doubt was beginning to gnaw at his confidence. They had looked in at the SeaVue, and then lurked about the community until it was clear that nothing more was going to happen. Johnson had been reluctant to leave, because that was tantamount to admitting that the whole operation had come to nothing, but finally he could delay no longer and they headed back toward St. John's.

One of the constables— Tremblay— sat on the seat beside him, half turned to chat with his colleague in the back. Their remarks were in French and apparently highly amusing, since they laughed frequently. In spite of endless weeks of language training Johnson could not follow their rapid Montreal *patois*, but he was sure they were talking about him. His neck and ears burned. He longed to order them to speak English, but was afraid that they would then say nothing at all, and the silence would make him appear even more ridiculous. He kept his eyes on the road and said nothing.

"Barker?"

"Yeah, Brewster?"

"These little old woods are harder to get through than they look, aren't they?"

"Were you in Nicaragua, Brewster?"

"No. Guatamala, though. Why?"

"I have been in Nicaragua, Honduras, and Zaire, and Cambodia, and a half a dozen other goddamn jungle places, and I have never in my whole life come in contact with anything like this. These aren't woods. It's a goddamn *hedge*."

"Funny. From the road it looked like you could just walk through. Oh, shit!"

"What?"

"Nothing new. Just a branch in the eye. Listen, do you think it might be easier if we headed up the hill a bit?"

Constables Wayslenchuk and Cameron, having monitored the traffic leaving St. Cyril's and given out a satisfactory number of tickets for missed stop signs, missing tail lights and unbuckled seat belts, collected hamburgers and plates of chips from Fong's Take-Out and wheeled into the gravel pit for a late supper. Their lights caught the lower halves of two bodies, half in and half out of the front doors of a parked car, with the heads and shoulders up under the dashboard. Constable Cameron's imagination, haunted by American cop shows on television, supplied a pool of blood and he spilled two cups of scalding coffee down his pant leg getting out of the cruiser.

After sorting out the two boys and relieving them of their pliers and screwdrivers, the two policemen withdrew to stand by their own car in conference.

"What the hell do we do now?" said Wayslenchuk, poking with his toe at the remains of a hamburger that had been stepped on in the confusion. "I've never seen electronic equipment like that. That thing's got radar, surveillance gear...."

"And that radio. God, they could talk to Moscow on that thing. What did those stupid kids think they were going to do with that? And who the hell does it belong to?"

"Listen," said Wayslenchuk. "Whoever it belongs to is probably somebody who isn't going to be too delighted that we've been looking at it, right? Could be CSIS, or— hell, I don't know, didn't Johnson have some fantasy about the Japanese Red Army or something? I don't buy that, but anybody who's got equipment like that is out of our league. We don't want to take responsibility for this. Johnson was at that meeting, and he was hanging around after. It's his kind of thing, not ours. I'm going to call it in, all right? Let him stick his neck out."

"Suits me," said Cameron. "And let's just hope that whoever owns that stuff doesn't get back until Johnson gets here."

Mr. Callahan and Miss Hiscock had stayed at the scene of the fire only long enough for Mr. Callahan to discharge his duty as a leading citizen of The Shore, pledging assistance for the rebuilding of the hall and promising the firemen that he would talk to his government contacts about new equipment. After that, however, they had not followed the pattern established over a number of recent evenings, and head for St. John's and a nightcap at the Crowsnest or a cup of tea at the Radisson. Instead, they drove slowly along The Shore and then parked at a quiet lookout point, engaged in serious conversation.

Their conclusion was not arrived at quickly or lightly. They both took their religions seriously, and although they knew that what used to be called "mixed marriages" were possible, neither was very sure of what the theological implications or liturgical arrangements might be. But once they had settled the main point, and agreed that they would each discuss the matter with their respective clergymen at the first opportunity, a sense of rising excitement began to take over.

Even so, when Mr. Callahan suddenly suggested that they should both go immediately and call on the parish priest, Miss Hiscock demurred. It was, as she pointed out, getting rather late. However, when he explained that he and Father Morrissey were old friends, and that they often called on one another late in the evening, she began to relent. And when he added with a shy, almost boyish grin that, anyway, he "couldn't wait to tell somebody the news" she could not resist.

Mr. Callahan started the car and headed back toward St. Cyril's. After a moment, he took his right hand off the wheel and placed it on the seat between them, palm upward. After another moment, Miss Hiscock placed her hand in his, and their fingers intertwined.

Constable Wayslenchuk's call crackled from the radio in Johnson's car, interrupting the flow of unintelligible banter between his two assistants. Johnson listened in rising excitement. The two young constables grabbed for handholds as he slammed the car into a tight U-turn and accelerated back over the road to St. Cyril's.

"All right, you guys," Johnson said. "This looks like what we've been waiting for. Laframboise, check out the weapons. And speak English, both of you."

"Brewster?"

"Yo."

"You wouldn't expect to find a sort of a swamp up here on a hillside like this, amongst all these trees, would you?"

"Man, it wouldn't surprise me to find a goddamn volcano. I paid a hundred and seventy-five dollars for these shoes in Washington just last week. Christ!"

"What?"

"Just give me a hand, here, will you, Barker? I've got my foot down in some kind of hole."

Bannister was growing desperate. The SeaVue had distracted Al for a while, but there had been no opportunity for Bannister to get away from him.

"This is a real interesting place," Al said finally, draining his beer. "I ain't seen nothing like it since about nineteen fifty-three. In Oklahoma. Well, looks like your contacts ain't coming, Bronco. Finish up your ginger ale and let's go."

"No, wait, Al. Listen. There's one more thing I got to do. You remember that priest at the meeting?"

"The little guy who was talking when the fire started? Say, he ain't the guy with the arm, is he?"

"For Chrissake, Al, I told you. That's a *place*. No, but that guy is another important contact. I got to see him tonight. Just give me about twenty minutes to run up the hill...."

"Look, Bannister," Al began in a voice that caused a few heads at neighbouring tables to turn, then checked himself with an effort. "Listen, I understand you're trying to do things right, but you can forget all that. I'm telling you, I'm going to handle everything. You don't need to worry any more." To himself he resolved that, Management Sensitivity or not, Bannister would get a thorough going over by the shrinks as soon as he could get him back to Houston.

"Yeah, Al, I appreciate it. But this is important. That little guy is a key to this whole operation. I've just gotta talk to him for a few minutes. He's...he's real cagey. If I don't have a word with him before I go, it could make things real rough for whoever takes over."

Al looked across the table narrowly. "Listen, you're not trying to sneak away and have a couple of drinks, are you? I can see how this place could have that effect on a guy, but surely you can see that for a man in your position...."

"No, dammit! I'm telling you, I just need to have a couple of minutes with that priest. If I don't, this whole operation could go up in smoke!"

"All right, all right. Take it easy. Don't get yourself excited. I'll drive you up there."

There were no options left. "Okay," Bannister said. "But I've got to see him alone. If anybody else is with me, he won't.... It won't work."

A few tables away, the People on the Left were still talking.

"...You know, the more I think about it the more I'm beginning to think that maybe Father Morrissey was onto something."

"Go 'way with you. He was just...."

"No, I think so, too. Remember how he came busting in, all agitated...."

"Right. And remember how he started off? 'Is it not true that Mogul Oil has designated the Hard Shore as an area of major development....' something like that. It really sounded as though he could have had some information."

"Oh, sure. And I suppose the CIA made the furnace blow up so he couldn't reveal it, right?"

"Come on, boy, I'm not that paranoid. But, all the same, he could have learned something. Priests hear all kinds of stuff. I think maybe we should drop in on him before we head home."

"Me too. He doesn't go to bed early, and he's always glad to see us."

"Oh, for God's sake!"

"Shut up, my son. You've just been out-voted. Anyway, what harm can it do? We'll finish our beer and head up there."

Jackie and Phonse, released with strict orders to report to RCMP headquarters next morning, drove aimlessly through town. "Jeez," said Phonse, slumped morosely in the passenger seat. "We're really in the shit this time, Jackie. We should of listened to Carm and Treece." Jackie didn't reply. "Where we goin' now?" Phonse asked.

Jackie had been pondering the same question, and had just made up his mind. "I don't know about you," he said, "but I believe I'm going to see Father Morrissey. He stays up late."

Phonse straightened up. "Father Morrissey? What the hell do you want to do that for?"

"I been thinkin'. Our mothers has got to find out about this sooner or later, right?" Phonse swallowed and looked even more miserable. "Now," said Jackie, "I ain't exactly lookin' forward to breakin' the news, right? I kind of figures Father Morrissey might do a better job of it."

Phonse brightened a little. "Hey, right! He'll believe almost anything. We could tell him...tell him we thought that car belonged to a friend of ours, right? And we was just...we was...maybe tryin' to fix it for them?"

"Let me do the talking," Jackie said. "I'll think of something."

Pete Kelly and the executive of the Development Association had retired to the SeaVue to discuss their next moves on the development front and the new problems posed by the destruction of the hall.

"All right," said the President. "So that's agreed. Pete will get in touch with Mogul Oil tomorrow. Too bad that P.R. fella wouldn't come in for a beer with us...."

"He didn't look well all evening," Kelly said. "Must be getting the flu. Anyway, I'll call him tomorrow."

"My God, did you ever see anything like poor Father?" said the Vice-president, hunching his shoulders to mimic a pop-eyed Father Morrissey arising from the mud puddle.

Kelly held up his hand to interrupt the roar of laughter. "That's a sin for us, to be laughin' behind his back. His feelings was already hurt at bein' left out of the meeting, and then to go down face and eyes in the mud, and everybody...." His voice broke, and there was another round of hilarity.

"All the same, though," Kelly said when he recovered his breath, "maybe we ought to go around and call on him, just to let him know we're thinking about him."

"You think so?"

"Yes, boy, why not? We can borrow a flask of rum from Johnny Dinn and go by and say we was just callin' in to see was he all right. We don't want him shaggin' up our development plans, but it's only right to show respect for the cloth."

"By God, you're right. Let's go."

At the gravel pit, Sergeant Johnson took over like a seasoned campaigner.

"Okay," he said. "Now, you say these kids told you that the occupants of the vehicle went into the woods over there. That right, Walenski?"

"Ah...I'm Cameron, Sergeant. That's Wayslenchuk over there. And, yeah, that's what they said."

"Right. And if somebody went through the woods in that direction, where would they be likely to come out?"

"Somewhere around the church, I suppose."

"That's what I figured. Okay. Now we're going to have to leave one man here— that's you, Wollenchick— with an automatic rifle and a shotgun, just in case those guys come back.

"...But I don't think they will," he added grimly, "because I think the rest of us will find them first. I just hope we're in time!"

"Brewster?"

"What the hell do you want?"

"No need to get sore. Is that lights I see up ahead? I think that's the back of the church. Only there seems to be a kind of a gully or something here."

"Yeah. We'd better try to go around front. It looks wet down there."

"Won't be long now. Listen, once we get the stuff, surely we could go back around by the road?"

"Sounds good to me."

When Father Morrissey had got back to his house, his mind was in a turmoil of excitement and frustration. Mrs. Fagan, of course, had gone home long since. He took off his muddy clothes in the back porch, put on old jeans and a sweatshirt, and slipped into the church. It took a considerable effort of will and half an hour of prayer and meditation to restore a measure of calm.

Next came a long, luxurious, hot bath. By that time, his stomach began to remind him of how little he had eaten earlier. In the kitchen he prepared one of the concoctions featuring melted cheese and pickles that he was allowed to make only when Mrs. Fagan was not around, and brewed a large pot of strong tea. When the last crumb was gone from his plate, he rolled a cigarette and leaned back. Body and soul restored, he began to think of the papers that had fallen so miraculously into his hands.

Brewster and Barker were pushing their way through the overgrown lilac bushes between the church and the clergy house. Suddenly Brewster stopped.

"Hold it."

"What?"

"A car just pulled up out front. Somebody's coming up the walk. Shit!"

"What?"

"I think it's that oil guy. Bannister. Jarvis said he might try something like this."

"Who?"

Brewster stepped forward onto the path. "Hey, you! Where do you think you're going?"

"Oh, my God! You scared me. Who the hell are you? Oh, I get it. You're Jarvis's boys. Well, listen...."

Al had seen the encounter and got out of the car. "What's going on, Bronco? Who are these guys?"

"They're...ah...Jarvis's boys, Al. I think."

"What? CIA? Here? What the hell...Bannister, if you've got some scam going with the CIA, I'm going to...."

"Shhh! For Chrissake, man! You'll wake up the whole town!"

"Don't tell me to shush, you goddamn CIA assho...."

"Hey, Brewster!"

"What?"

"Another car just pulled up. It's two kids. Hello, boys. Where are you going?"

"Just going to see Father."

"Yeah? What are you, altar boys or something?"

"Used to be," said Phonse, a little shamefacedly.

"Is that so? Well listen, boys, Father Whatsisname is busy right now.... Holy shit! I don't believe it!"

"What?"

"Two cars this time. There's about ten people coming. Ah...good evening, folks...."

Al rounded on Brewster again. "What is this? Reinforcements from Miami? You guys planning another Bay of Pigs?"

"Ah, shut up! If it wasn't for you goddamn rig-pushing amateurs...."

Jackie and Phonse were edging toward the gate as Mr. Callahan and Miss Hiscock arrived.

"Good evening, Jackie, Phonse. What are you doing here? And who are all these people? Has something happened to Father Morrissey?"

"Evening, Mr. Callahan. Ma'm. I don't know, sir. We was just passin' by...." The boys sidled toward the gate again, only to find their way blocked by the executive committee of the Development Association. Pete Kelly pushed them aside as he came forward.

"Mr. Callahan! What's going on?"

The shouting match between Brewster and Al had increased in volume and intensity, and now included Barker and Bannister. The People on the Left, always ready for a good argument, especially if it involved references to such topics as the CIA and oil development, were beginning to join in.

"Just a minute, Pete." Mr. Callahan pushed through the milling crowd, put a hand on Al's shoulder and spun him around. "Look here," he said, "just keep your voice down and watch your language. There's a lady present, and you are in front of a priest's house!"

"What? Who the hell are you? By God, nobody tells me...."

"Al! Wait...!"

The babble of voices was building toward a crescendo as Sergeant Johnson and his small command rounded the corner by the church.

"Sound like some kinds of riot!" said Laframboise.

"Unbutton your holsters," said Johnson, "but nobody draws his gun until I give the order. We'll take them by surprise."

Inside, Father Morrissey had taken the papers from their hiding place in his big Oxford Dictionary and carried them to his desk, where another steaming mug of tea sat waiting. Carefully, he smoothed the strange, crinkly sheets out on his old desk blotter, familiarly pitted and scarred by burning tobacco shreds. He was briefly distracted by the sound of voices outside, but just as he was about to go to the window the noise seemed to die away.

Leaning over the papers avidly, he tucked a newly-rolled cigarette into the corner of his mouth and reached for a match.

Printed in Canada